Stories
from
The Great War Vol. I

The Pooley Miners

Mick Manise

GHP

**Grosvenor House
Publishing Limited**

This book is published by
Grosvenor House Publishing Ltd
Link House
140 The Broadway, Tolworth, Surrey, KT6 7HT.
www.grosvenorhousepublishing.co.uk

A CIP record for this book
is available from the British Library

ISBN 978-1-78623-206-9

THIS PILLAR OF SEVERANCE
IS ERECTED BY THE WORKPEOPLE
AND OWNERS OF POOLEY HALL
COLLIERY TO THE UNDYING
MEMORY OF THOSE FROM THIS MINE
WHO ANSWERED THE NATION'S CALL
AND FELL IN THE GREAT WAR
1914 – 1919

Ball Albert E
Booton Sydney C.
Collins Thomas
Congrave John P.
Cope William E.
Daft Frank
Dean Williams
Frost Thomas H.
Harper Thomas
Hennesey James
Hedges Zachariah
Houghton Charles
Jackson Arthur
Jacobs William
Lees Frank R.
Nash Charles

Owen Arthur H.
Perry Frank D.
Pallett George
Prince Jack W.
Riley Charles E.
Startin Frank
Storer Oliver
Such J. Edward
Talbot Joseph
Turner George F.
Wood Sydney
Welbourne Samuel
West William
Williams Clive
Willis Percy
Willis Samuel

Who stands if freedom fall?
Who dies if England Live?

By the same author

Captain Desmond Ellis Hubble
(From Cradle to Grave)

John Banner
(His Life & Times)

Harry Bunn's War

mickmanisebooks.uk
Mickmanise@copyright2017

Dedication

To my wife, Christine
Thank you for putting up with me!

Acknowledgements

Yet again, many thanks to Jan Lowe for her terrier like research, Ann Bowmen of Polesworth whose research regarding the Pooley Hall Memorial made this book possible, Simon Westwood for his proof reading skills and my very good friend Graham Bennett for his advice on all things pictorial. D.P. & G. Military Publishers for their kind consent to reproduce maps. Father Philip of Polesworth Abbey for the kind words in his foreword. The people whose brains I have picked are many and I apologise if I have forgotten anyone; Ken Marlow and Simon Westwood, photography, Peter Evans, Tim Thurlow, Sean and Kevin Little, whose knowledge of all things World War I never ceases to amaze me. Thanks are due to all those family and friends whose encouragement is a driving force. Andy Gammon, for his kind permission to reproduce his sketch of tunnel activity.

All have gladly donated their time or skills for the benefit of the Royal British Legion.

Sources

The following are a mix of quoted or inspirational sources:

Public Records

National Archives

The Long, Long Trail

The Great War Forum

The 11th Royal Warwicks in France 1915-16 by Brevet Colonel C.S. Collison, DSO

On The Trail of the Great War, Birmingham: 1914-1918 by Alan Tucker

World WarIGas Warfare Tactics and Equipment by Simon Jones.

The First Day on the Somme by Martin Middlebrook

The War that Ended Peace by Margaret MacMillan

Somewhere in France by William and Geoffrey Whittaker

Beneath Flanders Fields, the tunnellers' war 1914-18 by Peter Barton, Peter Doyle and Johan Vanderwalle.

Polesworth Library

Pooley Country Park Visitor Centre.

Quotes from the Battalion war diaries are reproduced in italics and unchanged by interpretation or grammar.

All information gleaned from the internet has been verified from another source.

Introduction

Located on the narrow lane leading to Pooley Country Park, Polesworth, stands a World War I memorial set back from the road in its own fenced off area on the left-hand side. It is unusual to see such memorials in a remote location as they are normally placed in churchyards or in places reflecting the community's personal loss. On closer inspection this memorial reveals that it was once part of a thriving community. The memorial was commissioned by the owners of Pooley Hall Colliery after World War I to reflect the loss and to honour those miners who had made the ultimate sacrifice to King and country. The memorial contains 32 names engraved on the side faces and these men are honoured each year on 11th November by the Royal British Legion and local people.

Polesworth is a large village with a population allowing it the potential status of Market Town and is situated in the county of Warwickshire, but close to borders with Staffordshire, Derbyshire and Leicestershire. The village origins are probably related to the building of the Abbey in the 9th century by Saint Modwena. The first Abbess was known as Edgytha and gives name to the church on the same site, St Editha's. The name Polesworth is from the Saxon words, pol meaning pool and worth meaning dwelling, the village is built on the River Anker at a point where there is a shallow crossing. Polesworth has many aspects which reflect English history from the Iron Age, through the Roman occupation, to the Reformation and the Industrial Revolution.

As with much of England, the Industrial Revolution changed the area and the mining of coal, along with products made from clay, became the main sources of local business and employment. Pooley Hall Colliery was privately owned and part of the Hall estate. There has been a brick manor house at this site since 1509, built by Sir Thomas Cockayne who was knighted by King Henry VII. The Hall stayed in the Cockayne family until it was sold due to the debt of Sir Anthony Cockayne, 1st Baronet, who sided with the Royalists during the English Civil War.

Coal had been taken from the Estate for hundreds of years as there were small seams near to the surface. The first deep shaft was sunk in 1847, not far from the main house. In 1897 the Pooley Hall Colliery was formed and stayed in private possession until the industry was nationalised in 1946, the mine eventually closed in 1965. One of the waste products from mining called Clod (carboniferous bind), was utilised in the making of bricks. The development of mining in the area created an expanding population and some villages were wholly mining communities. Sons followed fathers to the mines, some as young as twelve, where they were employed as Pit Boys running errands and generally making themselves useful until they were old enough to go underground. The concentration of miner communities was also due to the employee being entitled to a two or three bedroom house dependant on the size of his family. Quite often, where records are available a soldier's family address on enlistment is different to the address recorded when he became a casualty; the widow and children having lost the home provided by the colliery and returned to live with family. It was a dangerous, filthy way to earn a living, but men and their families were proud to be in the mining industry. Pooley Hall Colliery was the very first mine in England to provide Pit Head Baths, but this was not until 1926 when the Duke of York (later King George V1) visited the mine and spoke to miners. For the visit half a ton of whitewash had been used and a toilet with a rose wood seat placed at the bottom of the pit shaft. Needless to say, the miners were not allowed to use this facility until after the Duke's visit and then it created such a stench it had to be removed! None of the men featured in these stories ever experienced such workplace luxury and finished shift covered in coal dust and washed themselves and their clothes at home. Many of the men also joined Territorial Army units, such as the Tamworth Territorials, who with the start of War joined their Regiments and went off to fight. Many more men answered the call to arms and were posted to Battalions of the New Army and by 1916, with the pressing need for more manpower, conscription was introduced and more men sent to fight.

Due to the proximity of the area to the county borders, the Royal Warwickshire, North and South Staffordshire Regiments appear often in these stories and, unsurprisingly, some of the men's experience as miners was put to good use in the war below ground. Of the thirty two names on the memorial, thirty one men have been positively identified, but this book contains thirty three stories. I will leave the reason for the reader to determine if my logic is sound! Writing about these men is now purely from paper records; there are very few witnesses. The children of these men are now themselves very elderly and usually cannot contribute much detail as their fathers didn't talk about their experiences. Inevitably, there is repetition in the use of census and other public records, but in my opinion the story is not complete without a picture of where these men came from and what they had done.

Today, the land formerly forming the colliery is a country park. Scarred by open cast mining during World War 2, the land has been returned to nature and is a delightful place to visit and contemplate the sacrifice made by these men. The park is sixty two hectares, bordered by the Coventry Canal, approximately one third of the area is designated site of special scientific interest and is covered by woodland and lakes formed by mining subsidence.

The park would also be a wonderful place to sit on a sunny day and read this book, the royalties of which will be donated, as with all my works, to the Royal British Legion.

Thank you for your support.

Mick Manise

2017.

Cover Picture

I am very grateful for the cover design for this series of stories to my long time friend Graham Bennett of West Coast Media Solutions who has donated his services free of charge in order to support the Royal British Legion. (The Photographs used to create this cover are from the authors collection).

The three medals shown are one of the common characteristics of the stories as all subjects, regardless of their fate, earned at least two if not all three of them.

The Stars

The first medal to be authorised was the 1914 Star following relentless pressure from King George V who ardently believed that the men of 1914 deserved a distinctive award. The army resisted this move until late in 1917, believing that a simple clasp on a campaign medal would suffice as had previously been awarded, for instance, in the Boer War. 378,000 of this star were awarded for active service between 4th August and 22nd November 1914, most going to the original members of the British Expeditionary Force (BEF), sometimes known as 'The Old Contemptibles' following a derogatory remark made by the Kaiser who said that the BEF was a contemptible little army. The cut-off date for this medal was 22nd November 1914, which was determined to be the last day which satisfied the above criteria but also marked the stabilisation of the Western Front and the commencement of the static nature of that theatre of war.

There was some resentment from other branches, such as the Royal Navy who were at war at sea. The only members of the Senior Service who qualified, were some land based units manning artillery and port defences. The 1914 Star was then replaced by the 1914-15 Star (as shown in the cover picture), the medals are identical except that on the 1914 version, there is a scroll wound around the crossed Roman swords at the centre bearing the words, '*Aug-1914-1915*', whilst on the later version the scroll is shorter bearing the dates, '*1914-15*'. This medal was devised following some bad feeling from those who had served in 1914 but had not been entitled to the first award, such as the theatres of war not covered by the qualifying criteria and, as previously mentioned, the Royal Navy. The 1914-15 Star was awarded to those who had served in any theatre of war, regardless of military branch, between 23rd November 1914 and 31st December 1915. Some 2,366,000 1914-15 Stars were awarded and like the 1914 version they were always accompanied by the British War and Victory Medals, this was even to those killed during 1914-15 or whose wounds had curtailed their service.

The fact that the 1914-15 Star was almost identical to the 1914 Star then caused some resentment from the recipients of the latter who claimed they deserved a distinguishable award. To resolve this a dated clasp, (*5th Aug - 22nd Nov 1914*), was produced to be worn on the 1914 Star's ribbon which was awarded to those who had been at the front within range of the enemy's mobile artillery before midnight on 22nd November 1914. This was accompanied by a silver Rose to be worn on the ribbon bar of the medal.

The British War Medal

This circular silver medal was the basic award of World War I. It bears the Monarch's effigy and titles and would have been the award to carry individual clasps as previously awarded but not authorised for this conflict.

This medal was the only one of the four to be awarded on its own, for instance for those on duties around the Empire such as India. A bronze version of this medal was awarded to non-combatant servants or porters enlisted from Africa or India. The recipient's details were impressed around the edge including name, initials, abbreviated rank and unit. Approximately 6,500,000 BWM's were awarded making it the most common British campaign medal.

The Victory Medal

At the Versailles Conference of 1919 the Allies agreed on a standardised medal to be awarded to all those who had entered a theatre of war. The Victory medal was originally struck in dull bronze but later finished with a gold coating. The front has a simple Winged Victory figure and the reverse side the words, *"The Great War For Civilisation 1914-19"* in a wreath. Never awarded on its own, some 5,750,000 medals were distributed.

The medals were subsequently delivered in a small addressed cardboard box with the medal ribbon unattached and, in the case of a deceased soldier, to their nominated next of kin. The Rose and Clasp awarded with the 1914 Star was issued when applied for and that date recorded in the medal rolls for that regiment. The other awards common to all the soldiers killed, was the Memorial Plaque and Scroll. The idea for this was developed in 1916 and reflects the nation's overwhelming sense of loss which had been a feature of this terrible conflict. The Scroll was designed and worded by a committee set up to discuss the issue but the Plaque was a result of an open design competition offering a prize of £250 to the winner. The wording of the Scroll reflects the sacrifice made and the Plaque depicts Britannia in mourning offering a wreath with the British Lion and two dolphins to represent sea power. Around the front face are the words, *"He Died for Freedom and Honour"* and the name of the fallen person was printed in a frame. A small number with the wording commencing with 'She' were produced for eligible women casualties which included victims of U-boats at sea. The dates for eligibility were 4th August 1914 to 30thApril1920 to encompass those who died of wounds or disease after the war had concluded. 1,360,000 plaques were issued to the nominated next of kin to the subjects from Britain and the Empire.

The example above was kindly made available for use by Mr Tim Thurlow who has a collection of World War I artefacts which has taken over 30 years to accumulate; Tim is a Battlefield Guide and has been a valuable source for my research. Henry Blackstone, Corporal L10497, was serving with 7th Battalion the Queen's (Royal West Surrey Regiment) when he was killed on 10th August 1917 and is remembered at Tyne Cot Cemetery.

Foreword

Polesworth is unusual. In the aftermath of the Great War, two memorials were erected. One in the village near to the Abbey and another along Pooley Lane, the route that many took to the pithead, where miners from Polesworth and surrounding villages would pass. This second Polesworth memorial reminded those who walked that way, of those who had gone from their villages who had also worked at the Pooley Pit, and had not returned.

Though now not on a main route, the Pooley memorial remains very much part of the village. There is a commemoration each year at each of the war memorials and in recent years there has been a special service in the summer commemorating these miners from Pooley who gave their lives in times of war and the names that you'll find there and in this excellent book by Mick Manise. These men are not all from Polesworth, as those on the memorial by the Abbey are. They come from surrounding villages and belong here because of the mining heritage shared with the local communities.

I write here to commend this excellent book, *The Pooley Miners*; full of detail revealing the landscape of the time, recruiting, training and military discipline, and the theatres of war.

The familiar names of places and battles that have passed into our shared history and are being remembered again now, 100-years later, presented with the names of men from Polesworth and the villages around, who are also familiar to us and are recalled for their sacrifice at the service each year and at the Remembrance commemoration.

Miners no longer pass the Pooley memorial– the pit is long-since closed – yet here we are drawn into the lives of those who walked that way to the mine.

Mick Manise provides us with an insight into the story of those who are commemorated enabling us to walk with them and enter the heritage we share with them all.

This is a book for Polesworth and for the surrounding villages, a tribute to those we should not forget.

Father Philip Wells

Polesworth Abbey

Contents

Chapter 1

Why they were there

The causes of World War I are complex and who started the conflict is still a matter under debate, July 1914 in itself is covered by a number of books. Europe was divided into alliances of mutual understanding and interests, the Triple Alliance consisted of Germany, Austria-Hungary and Italy. Germany and Austria were natural allies, speaking the same language and were once the same nation; the Holy Roman Empire. Germany had a large army which was based on a conscription system where all able-bodied men served under arms and then were on a reserve status until aged 40, during that period they had to attend regular camps for training purposes. This system ensured that during times of conflict Germany could field an army where all its members were trained soldiers from day one. However, Germany's navy was weak. Austria was reliant on German might to assist with the troubles it was experiencing in its Balkan regions. Italy joined this alliance as she feared the threat that they presented on her northern boarders.

The Entente Cordiale consisted of France, Britain and Russia. France had a large land army but a small navy whilst Britain had the most powerful navy in the world but a small army. France feared the military build-up in Germany and sought the alliance with Great Britain which governed an empire stretching around the globe thereby controlling huge natural wealth and resources. Russia being so far from both countries seems a strange choice for an alliance but we need to look at the Royal families to understand why.

Queen Victoria of Great Britain and Empress of the British Empire with her husband Prince Albert had nine children. Eight of these children, either directly or by marriage, sat on the thrones of Great Britain, Prussia, Greece, Romania, Russia, Norway, Sweden and Spain. The descendants of this dynasty formed the Royal Families of Europe at the time of World War 1. Of the monarchs reigning in 1914, Kaiser Wilhelm II of Germany was the grandson of Victoria. His mother, also Victoria, was her eldest daughter. Wilhelm was not liked amongst his royal peers and by all accounts was a rude and arrogant man. Wilhelm's parents tried to educate him to the British attitudes to democracy but he resisted and followed the teachings of his tutors becoming Prussian and autocratic in his attitudes, he became estranged to an extent from his parents believing that they had Britain's interests at heart rather than Germany's.

The other family members related to Victoria were friendly to one another and this led to the Alliance between Great Britain and Russia, this also sent a message to Germany, at a time where it was the most powerful country of mainland Europe, that it now had two very large armies on its borders which would mean that any aggression would create a war on two fronts. It was hoped that this would provide an adequate deterrent against future aggression. Amongst other related alliances and treaties, Britain had also promised to protect Belgium.

Another factor governing the political situation in Europe was the emerging dissatisfaction of the working classes with their lot in life. Revolution was planned and bubbling and in most countries the issue was merely suppressed with military power. Britain alone was changing to a more democratic system with greater consideration given to workers' rights and welfare. This and future actions by Britain's Royal family ensured its survival at a time where most of Europe's Royal houses were falling or under threat. This revolutionary movement was active in the Balkans which desired independence from Austria.

On Sunday 28th June 1914 in Sarajevo, Arch Duke Franz Ferdinand, heir presumptive to the throne of the Austro-Hungarian Empire, was shot to death in his car along with his wife Sophia. The assassination was the second attempt of the day as earlier a grenade was thrown at his car, but missed, falling behind the vehicle and causing injury to onlookers. The successful assassin was a 19 year old Bosnian, Gavrilo Princip, a member of a movement called the Black Hand Gang. Princip had been party to the original attempt and following its failure had retired to a café, whilst sitting there he noticed the Royal car making a turn outside to resume its journey, the Royal coupe having been to the hospital to see the wounded from the hand grenade incident, taking the initiative Princip stepped out of the café and shot Sophia in the abdomen, he then shot Ferdinand in the neck. The latter died within minutes and Sophia on the way to hospital, this assassination started a series of events which ultimately led to war.

A month of political manoeuvring took place between Britain, France, Germany, Russia and Austria-Hungary known as the July Crisis and resulted in Austria-Hungary presenting Serbia with the 'July Ultimatum', a ten point demand purposely unacceptable to Serbia as the intention was to provoke war. The following day Russia ordered a partial mobilisation of land and sea forces in support of Serbia who responded to the ultimatum offering concessions which were rejected by Austria-Hungary who then declared war on Serbia on 28th July 1914. On 30th July Russia, in support of Serbia, ordered a general mobilisation against Germany. Kaiser Wilhelm asked his cousin Tsar Nicholas II to cease all military mobilisations and also asked France to remain neutral. When Russia ignored the Kaiser's request, Germany mobilised and declared war on Russia on 1st August 1914. France ordered its military forces to retire six miles from the border with Germany to prevent incidents, mobilised its reserves but ignored Germany's request for neutrality. Germany attacked Luxemburg on 2nd August and declared war on France the following day. On 4th August Belgium refused a request to allow German forces to cross its borders to attack France and Germany declared war on Belgium and attacked anyway. Great Britain had demanded that Belgium neutrality be respected and following an unsatisfactory response to its ultimatum in that respect, declared war on Germany taking effect from 11 p.m., 4th August 1914.

Under its obligation to the Entente Cordial, Britain dispatched an Expeditionary Force (BEF) consisting of six infantry divisions and five cavalry brigades under the command of Field Marshall Sir John French to Northern France.

Chapter 2

Albert Edward Ball

Entry 284, page 36, of St Editha's Parish record of baptisms for the year 1885, relate to the child of John and Kate Ball, Albert Edward Ball, who was born on August 7th of that year. The family lived at Moulds Yard Tamworth, an address long gone now but described as an open courtyard near to the Old Stone Cross Pub and the family head, John, was a miner.

By 1901 the family had expanded to five. Albert now 16, probably left school at the age of 12. He had two younger brothers and was employed as a labourer at a local paper mill. There are two rivers running through Tamworth; the Tame and the Anker. These rivers supported a variety of industries such as Corn Mills,two paper mills, print works and woollen manufacture.

In 1907, Albert married Ada Georgina Preston in Hackney London. He was now employed as a Constable with the Metropolitan Police Service and still was in 1911, living at 128 Glenarm Road Clapham N.E. London. By now there was an addition to Albert and Ada's family; a boy, Henry John Ball, three years old.

On 16th March 1917, Albert complied with the instructions of his conscription orders and attended the Royal Citadel, Plymouth, the home base of 3 depot, Royal Garrison Artillery

(RGA). Albert had moved his wife and son to be near his own family in Tamworth and they were now housed at 385, Main Road, Glascote.

Somewhere between leaving school and his employments as a labourer at the paper mill, as a police officer in London and his join up date in 1917, Albert had been employed at Pooley Hall Colliery in one capacity or another. His army file records he was late of the Metropolitan Police Service indicating this was his last employer. The chances are he worked at the Colliery between leaving school and working at the paper mill, as his father was a miner and may well have arranged for him to take up employment with him.

Police Constable Albert Ball of the Metropolitan Police Service was subjected to the usual medical where he was declared classification A, fit for military service, and became Gunner 145245 A Ball of the Royal Garrison Artillery. The RGA was formed by royal warrant on 1st June 1899 when the mounted and dismounted branches of the Royal Artillery should be separated into two separate corps to be named the Royal Horse Artillery plus Royal Field Artillery and the Royal Garrison Artillery. Its main function, prior to World War 1, was the defence of the country via fortifications, in particular coastal defences such as the Royal Citadel at Plymouth. The RGA's role during the First World War was the creation of fixed artillery locations far back from the front line. It developed the use of heavy, long range artillery pieces from locations with no visual connection to targets. As the war progressed, so too did the techniques for target acquisition and the ground spotters at or in front of the front line, were supplemented with Royal Flying Corps spotters sending messages to the artillery command via wireless telegraphy.

Albert's training was brief. From 16th March to 1st April 1917, was spent at the Citadel. On 2nd April he was posted to the

RGA training camp at Bexhill-on-Sea; part of No. 1 Reinforcing Depot, Siege Artillery. On 12th May 1917 he was posted to the First Army Pool, part of the BEF in France, and arrived at his unit in the field on 31st May 1917.

The 137th Heavy Battery which Albert was posted to had arrived in France in April 1916 and was armed with six x 60 pounder artillery pieces. At the start of the war the batteries of the RGA were equipped with only four of these guns, and they were assigned to Infantry divisions. This changed and batteries were combined to form heavy artillery groups (HAG); the increase to six guns was implemented in 1916. The HAG which Albert joined was based at Grenay, west of Mons, and called the Lewis Group, 15 HAG. It comprised five batteries; 136th, 137th Heavy Batteries (both armed with the 60 pounders) and three Siege Batteries; 102nd, 308th (armed with 6" Howitzers) and 175th (armed with 9.2" Howitzers).

The only diary entry for the 137th is from the 6th to the 11th October 1917, where is recorded that it was leaving the 1st Army area and being disbanded and redeployed. The 136th, 137th and 102 heavy batteries, were transferred to the 2nd Canadian HAG and left to join their new hosts on the 6thOctober 1917. Between 6a.m.and 12noon on the 7thOctober,the guns of the 137th fired 20 rounds at Harnes Church approximately 12 kilometres away and a likely site for an artillery observation post. On the 8th, 9th and 10th October 1917, the diary records that all batteries were involved in harassing and destructive shoots. Harassing fire was by no means a new concept but due to the availability of large quantities and cheapness of high explosive, the practise was developed to an art. The basic concept was to deny the enemy the opportunity to rest or sleep and thereby increase the effects of shell shock and sleep deprivation on the enemy's health and morale. Destructive fire is self-defining but would require a greater degree of accuracy to achieve its objective.

On 1st March 1918, Albert commenced 14 days leave and travelled home to Tamworth to see his wife and son for the last time, on 25thMarch he dutifully reported back to his unit in the field. On 2nd November 1918 Albert reported sick and was removed to 20th Casualty Clearing Station, he died on 3rd November 1918,eight days before the fighting ceased. His cause of death was recorded as *'Died from Pneumonia due to exposure whilst on military duty'*.

Albert's death was related to the Great Flu Pandemic of 1918 which ravaged the world's population between January 1918 and December 1920 and resulted in between 20,000,000and 50,000,000deaths. A feature of this tragedy is that illnesses of this nature usually cause most deaths in vulnerable groups, under two years, over 70 years and those with a weakened immune system. This strain of flu attacked healthy adults and was widely spread by the movement of troops by train and ship. Albert's death would coincide with the second wave of the disease which was particularly deadly and started in August 1918 in France, Africa and the USA. In fast progressing cases such as Albert's, death was commonly caused by Pneumonia. Influenza normally appears in two strains, one mild the other more serious. Normally the least serious strain is spread because the severely affected stay at home whilst those not as poorly go to work and spread their germs via coughing and sneezing. In 1918 the norm was reversed, those not so poorly stayed in the trenches whilst those severely affected were loaded to trains, transported to hospitals and thereby spread the more virulent form.

On admission to hospital on 2ndNovember, it was immediately apparent that Albert was dying. A telegram was immediately sent to his wife Ada, informing her that her husband was very ill but regrettably it would not be possible for her to visit him. This was no doubt due to the medical profession now realising that there was an extremely serious situation which they had to make every effort to control but, as we now know, it was too late. The following day a second telegram was sent notifying Ada of her husband's death and the cause. The whole family must have been sent into a state of shock. They had lived with the fear of losing Albert since he went to France in 1917 and for him, a healthy man, to be taken in such cruel circumstances so close to the end must have been a bitter pill to swallow. There was no joy and celebration in the Ball households on or after the 11th November.

It appears from the records that Ada Ball now had to fight for everything. A record of correspondence has survived where she asks, for a death certificate in order to apply for financial assistance for her and her son. In January 1919 the ministry of pensions issued a certificate enabling Ada to be considered for a pension, it is not clear whether this was granted. On 14th February 1919, the register of soldier's effects recorded that Albert's wealth was £7.5s.5p and on 19th December 1919 this was enhanced by a £7 War Gratuity; both payable to Ada as the sole legatee. Albert's possessions were sent to Ada and included letters, photos, wallet, razor, scissors, belts and a pencil case.

Albert was buried in Plot: I. E. 17 Premont British Military Cemetery, Picardie, France and was awarded the British War and Victory Medals.

Chapter 3

Sydney Curson Booton

Sydney was born in 1893, the third child of Frank and Abigail Booton of Austry Road, Warton, Tamworth. Frank was a Waggoner on a farm and when he left school, Sydney followed him into the same profession. In 1911, Sydney is recorded as living as a lodger with the family of George Frisby and was in fact his servant, employed still as a Waggoner. At a stage between 1911 and 1916, Sydney changed professions and was employed at Pooley Hall Colliery. In what capacity is not known but he was likely to be using his skills as a Waggoner to haul the mined coal, above or below ground.

There are few records to tell us when Sydney joined the army but he enlisted at Atherstone and did not serve abroad until after 1st January 1916 and this service was with the 2nd Battalion Royal Warwickshire Regiment which had been in France since October 1914. In all probability, Sydney was conscripted after January 1916, the Military Service Act of 27th January 1916, brought conscription into effect and applied to every British male subject who on 15 August 1915 was ordinarily resident in Great Britain, who had attained the age of 19 but was not yet 41 and on 2ndNovember 1915, was unmarried or a widower without dependent children. There were of course certain but few exceptions; health grounds, being unfit or previously rejected for service for health reasons or being a religious minister. Sydney completed basic training either with 3rd (Reserve) or 4th (Extra Reserve) Battalions of the Royal Warwickshire Regiment before being posted to France and joining 2nd Battalion there.

The only other fact currently known about Joseph is that he was killed on 9th October 1917 whilst serving as Private 24404 Booton, aged 24, with the 2nd Battalion. On that date the Battalion was engaged in the Battle of Passchendaele, otherwise known as the third battle of Ypres. Ypres is a City in Belgium which had been a neutral country since the Treaty of London in 1839; Germany's invasion of Belgium was the reason Great Britain declared war in 1914. The City of Ypres had been successfully kept from falling into German hands. Their original intention had been to drive through the BEF to the coast, to gain the use of the ports there. Having failed in those original objectives, the German Army sought to capture the City to create a local victory. The first battle in 1914 had cost them 160,000 casualties. The war in this sector became static but the front had formed a Salient around Ypres and the German forces effectively surrounded it on three sides much of it being high ground from where they could bombard the salient and its occupants with artillery. The City was gradually reduced to rubble and became very costly to defend, but the attitude to this was simply that it would not honour those who had fallen in the defence of the city to then give it up. The second battle of Ypres was an attack by the German army between 22nd April and 15th May 1915, again the Salient was held but at a cost. The Third battle was planned for, and executed between, 31st July and10th November 1917 by the British and French commands with the intention of destroying

German forces in Flanders, gaining control of the high ridges South and East of Ypres, capture Passchendaele and a vital railway junction for supplying the German army in the area.

The first phase of the offensive commenced on 31st July at 3.50 a.m. and involved four main battles; battle of Pilckhem Ridge, capture of Westhoek, battle of Hill 70 and the battle of Langemarck. The second phase occurred between September and October 1917 and although the German defences had managed to prevent the British from attaining all its objectives so far, the weather and ground conditions had added a high sickness toll to the already high casualty rate experienced and the manpower shortage became of serious concern. The third phase commenced on 9th October 1917 and on the 7th, twodays before the battle started, the 2nd Battalion Royal Warwickshire Regiment, formed up into the front-line, East of Polygon Wood. The following day, tapes were run out in preparation for the coming attack to guide the men towards their objectives.

At 5.30 a.m. on 9th October 1917, the Battalion attacked the German positions to their front, A Company held the line, whilst D and C attacked with B Company in support. Messages flowed back to Battalion HQ throughout the day, brought by the wounded. Enemy machine guns were active, having to be individually dealt with and at 5.45 p.m. the attacking Companies sent up an SOS as the German artillery was laying down a heavy barrage on their positions. It was during this artillery part of the action that Sydney was killed, the Battalion fought on through the night of the 9th and the following day, 10th October 1917, they were relieved at 11 p.m. and retired to a camp. Casualties for this action were; six officers and 54 other ranks killed, six officers and 188 other ranks wounded, 70 other ranks missing (including Sydney), five other ranks died of wounds and two cases of shell shock.

Sydney's name was engraved on the Tyne Cot Memorial and he was subsequently awarded the British War and Victory Medals.

Chapter 4

Thomas Collins

Thomas was born in 1894 in Tamworth into a family with a background in the mining community. Thomas's father, John, was an Irishman from Portobello on the East Coast of the Emerald Isle and employed as an underground Stallman in a local coal mine. His mother, Ellen Collins, was a local girl from Burton in Staffordshire and worked from home as a Tailoress (as stated on the Census form) when not looking after her considerable family. In 1901, the family were resident at 4, Eaton's Yard, Lichfield Street, Tamworth and consisted of seven children; three girls and four boys of which Thomas was the second youngest. By 1911, the family had moved to16, Market Street, Tamworth and consisted of just three children, Ellen had successfully given birth to 14 children but to this point, only seven had survived. John Collins was now employed as a Holer and both sons were living at home; Thomas and his elder brother, Owen, were employed as below ground Pony Drivers. Also living with the Collins family are seven single men boarders and Ellen is employed 'at home'. She was supplementing the family income by renting her spare rooms out. The boarders were a mixture of Irishmen and Englishmen with professions such as miners, groom and general labourers. Ellen's youngest child, Rose Ann, at 13, was still at school; the extra income would have been very useful to keep a child at school after the legal age of 12.

Very few records exist in respect of Thomas but he went to France to serve with the 1st Battalion North Staffordshire Regiment, arriving in that country on 3rd December 1914. The 1st Battalion was stationed in Buttevant, Ireland, at the outbreak of World War I and returned to England to be mobilised to France. The Battalion disembarked at St Nazaire on 12th September 1914. The fact that Thomas was mobilised to France later, and that he got there so soon after the Battalion, would suggest that he was a trained soldier, there being insufficient time for him to be a recruit and complete basic training before being sent overseas. He was too young at 20 to be a time served soldier and was probably a reservist whose call up arrived after the Battalion mobilised and he caught up with them later. The diary does mention one absentee and four men unfit to travel. Thomas may have been one of the latter and joined his Battalion when his health improved.

Thomas joined the 1st Battalion in the trenches at Rue de Bois, on 23rd December 1914. The Battalion had been in the line since 12th December and it had been raining heavily. Despite the men's continual work to improve conditions, the trenches were knee deep in water and mud, moving about was made more difficult by planking floating in the water and the German's attention to the parapet with machine gun fire. This fire was a constant danger but also damaged the parapet reducing its defensive capability and filling the trench up with dirt. The constant rain had also washed out the graves of men buried on the Battalion's last turn in this trench system and corpses were floating in the trenches. The German front line was a mere 40 yards away from the British line at this location but this did not stop the German artillery from shelling the British trenches despite the danger of a shell falling short endangering their own troops. Snipers were a constant menace and a regular list of casualties from both sources was experienced.

On Christmas Eve, the diary records that the Germans requested an armistice for Christmas;

24ᵗʰ Dec.

Quiet Germans ask for armistice for Xmas. Sing songs in turn from opposite parapets. Germans win prize at this.

Xmas Day. 25ᵗʰ Dec.

Not a shot fired. The Germans bury their dead our men go and help. Baccy and cigars exchanged and Germans and our men walk about in the open together!! Return to the trenches at 4pm. Peace reigns till midnight.

26ᵗʰ Dec.

Germans still anxious to continue peace. No shots fired. Rain in Torrents.

27ᵗʰ Dec.

All quiet. Fearful storm. Trenches waist deep in water. Have to get outside in places.

28ᵗʰ Dec.

Rain awful trenches impossible try to make new trenches but fill at once.

29ᵗʰ Dec.

Another gale. Water rises everywhere.

30ᵗʰ Dec.

V. quiet day. Trenches Impossible.

The following day, New Year's Eve 1914, the Battalion left the front line and went into billets in Chapelle d'Armentières. The billets were dirty due to the constant use by men wet and covered in mud, but at least they had a roof over their heads and a stove to dry out in front of. After such a long tour in the front line it would be not unreasonable for the men to rest but the following day, 1ˢᵗ January 1915, working parties were found to carry timber for the Royal Fusiliers. The wet weather continued.

The Christmas Truce of 1914 has become a famous incident and following the event, the high commands of the forces concerned were not impressed by the soldiers' fraternisation and instructions were sent out that this was not to happen again. Calling for a temporary ceasefire was not an uncommon event however and were often called to allow the burial of the dead, it was the scale of the event that has made it so historically famous. All along the Western Front similar events took place but not in all; some places continued fighting. In the places where ceasefires occurred, various things were done; the most famous being the playing of football games. It was a time when enemies could stand together, share a smoke, show photos and remind themselves of their humanity. In 1915 the same was attempted but only in a few places was the non-fraternisation policy ignored. By 1916 the hatred between the opposing sides prevented anything of the sort, the gas attacks, wholesale slaughter and mining operations by both sides had quelled any desires for friendliness.

By June 1916 Thomas was serving as Lance Corporal (8049). There is no record of when he was promoted and he may have held that rank at the beginning of the war. Between Christmas 1914 and June 1916, the Battalion had been involved in action at Hooge and two large scale German gas attacks at Wulverghem during 1915. Thomas had survived some of the fiercest fighting of the war and now found himself on the side-lines for the great offensive of 1916, the Battle of the Somme.

In October 1915, the 1ˢᵗ Battalion North Staffordshire Regiment had been transferred to 72nd Brigade in 24th Division and, at the end of July 1916, entrained to billets at Morlancourt near to

Albert. The first part of August 1916 was spent training and on 4th they were addressed by the Divisional Commander, Major General Capper, to prepare them for participation in the Battle. After a stirring motivational speech, he reminded them of three important priorities; water, ammunition and communications. Water was a precious commodity and they must use it sparingly, trench warfare had allowed the men to be extravagant with the use of small arms ammunition (SAA) and they must 'unlearn' that. Finally communication; terrible mistakes had occurred by the failure to keep those at the rear informed of developments in the front. The reality with the first two issues was the problems with supply; a headache for those at the rear, and an even worse problem for those at the front running out of either. The lack of communication had exposed the inadequacies of commanding from the rear.

The 1st Battalion went into the line on 10th August to relieve 1/10th Liverpool Scottish near to La Briqueterie. They were occupying a series of funk holes (a scraping at the side of a trench which soldiers could cover with a tarpaulin to shelter from inclement weather) and trenches. They held these positions until 17th August when they were relieved to go to assembly areas to take part in a forthcoming battle. On this day, Captain A. J. Waugh RAMC was killed by a stray shell; this officer had been with the Battalion since November 1914 and was a huge loss to them. The stage of the offensive that Thomas and his comrades were to participate in, was the Battle of Delville Wood which had started on 14th July. The objective was to secure the British right flank whilst the centre of the offensive continued to take higher locations such as Pozières and High Wood. These higher positions were advantageous for artillery observation and start points for infantry attack.

On 30th August 1916 during the evening, the Battalion relieved 9th Rifle Brigade in positions in Delville Wood. Early on 31st August, the Germans commenced a heavy artillery bombardment on the Battalion's positions. This continued for five hours and at 11.45 a.m. Captain G.D. Chew sent the following message to Battalion HQ;

> *German bombardment has lasted nearly 5 hours. We have suffered heavy casualties. Our guns do not seem to be replying much. We have for certain 12 killed and about 25 wounded already.*

The message was delivered by a Private Moorcroft, as the Captain's regular runner was wounded and lying in the trench. The barrage was followed by an infantry attack on the South Staffordshire Battalion adjoining their positions. This attack was defeated with bombing by Battalions, Stokes Mortar, Lewis Gun and rifle fire. This was repeated throughout the day, the objective to dislodge the British forces from Delville Wood met with limited success and heavy casualties on both sides. At 12 midnight, the Adjutant sent a message stating that all was quiet and the Battalion were then relieved. Unusually, there is no casualty count for this action but from the messages sent back it is clearly high, particularly from shelling.

Thomas was killed this day and his body never recovered or identified, his name was subsequently carved on pier and face 14B and 14C of the Thiepval Memorial. He was awarded the 1914-15 Star, the Victory and British War Medals. (Although he had entered France in 1914, it was after the cut-off date for the 1914 Star).

Chapter 5

John Congrave

John was baptised John James Patrick Congrave on 11th August 1895, at Polesworth, which at that time was in the County of Warwickshire but the Diocese of Worcester. Tamworth is a town on the border of both Warwickshire and Staffordshire and very near to Leicestershire. These boundaries have changed over the years, sometimes causing confusion. John was born on 2nd June 1895, the eldest child of Charles and Clara Congrave. Charles was a bricklayer by profession. By 1901, the family had expanded to four sons and they were resident at Hall End, Polesworth. The 1911 census shows that the family were now resident at 41, High Street, Polesworth and, in addition to the four boys; Clara had given birth to two daughters. One other child had been born alive, but had died before this record was made. Charles now describes himself as a Journeyman Bricklayer; Journeyman being a title used by tradesmen who had long experience of their profession. The eldest three boys aged from 12 to 15 were in employment, a good indicator that John, now employed as an Above Ground Pit Boy in the Coal Mining Industry, had left school at the earliest age of 12. He was probably working at Pooley Hall Colliery where we know he was employed at some stage prior to his military service.

At the outbreak of war, John was 19 years old and eligible to volunteer for military service; his file did not survive the fires of World War II and the only document available to determine when he joined is his medal card. He was not eligible for the 1914 Star which was awarded for active service in 1914 until 22nd November that year and realistically only awarded to soldiers serving at the outbreak of War who were mobilised immediately. He joined the Royal Warwickshire Regiment as Private 16380 and was successively posted to the 2nd, 1st, 11th and then the 10th (Service) Battalions, all these Battalions had been mobilised to France either in 1914, in the case of the Regular units, or in 1915 in the case of the Service Battalion. If John had been serving at that time, he would have been eligible for the 1915 Star. Whenever John did join his Battalion in France, it was after 1st January 1916 and it is most likely he was a conscript, records do show, however, that he was enlisted at Atherstone, Warwickshire.

John was killed in action on 21st March 1918 at the age of 22. Unfortunately the Battalion war diary is complete for the whole war apart from the month of March 1918 which is missing. It is pure speculation to determine when he joined the Battalion and how he died; he may have survived the carnage of the Battle of the Somme or joined his unit the day before. The only clue as to what happened to John is that his body was not recovered or identified in the diary entries for either side of March 1918. Before March 1918 the Battalion had spent a lengthy period out of the line training and, during April 1918, the Battalion went back into trenches at Kemmel on the usual rotation basis. There was no attacking activity from either side during the relevant period and the most likely way John met his end was holding the front line at Kemmel and being subject to a direct hit from an artillery shell which left nothing of him to identify.

John's name was engraved on panel 3 of the Arras Memorial in Faubourg-d'Amiens Cemetery and he was awarded the British War and Victory Medals.

Chapter 6

William Ernest Cope

Little is known about William, but he was born in Alvecote in 1898 to Harry and Mary Cope, both of whom were born in Sheepy Magna, Leicestershire. In 1901 Harry, a Horse Carter on a farm, housed his family at 2, Lodge Farm Cottages, Hodge Lane, Tamworth. William, now three had a baby sister, Elsie, who was one year old. By 1911, the family had moved to The Green, Amington, Tamworth. Mary had given birth to five children. William, the eldest, was now 13 years old and still in school and the youngest, Harry, was three.

Sometime between the 1911 census and October 1918, William was employed at Pooley Hall Colliery, in an unknown capacity, and he joined the army. The only available information is his medal card and the entry in the register of effects relating to him. William was born in the second quarter of 1898, which made him 18 and eligible for overseas service on his 18th birthday which occurred in the spring of 1916. The allocation of his army number would coincide with April 1917, but this is not an accurate yardstick as numbers were sometimes changed. Whenever it was, he went to France and served as Gunner 152733 with 164th Siege Battery, Royal Garrison Artillery (RGA), which had been formed and sent to France in September 1916.

Siege Batteries of the RGA were equipped with heavy howitzers; usually 6, 8 and 9.2 inch howitzers which sent large calibre high explosive shells in high trajectory, plunging fire. Some batteries were equipped with huge railway or road mounted 12 inch howitzers. As the war progressed and artillery tactics were refined, the Siege Batteries were most often employed in destroying or neutralising the enemy artillery, as well as putting destructive fire down on strong points, dumps, store, roads and railways behind enemy lines.

During October 1918, William became unfit for duty due to sickness and was transported to 32nd Stationary Hospital, Wimereux, France, where he died on 31st October 1918. William was a victim of the Influenza Pandemic of 1918 which has been described in a previous story. William was buried in Terlincthun British Cemetery, Wimille, France. He left £12.0s.5d, supplemented by a War Gratuity of £6.10s.0d to his father Harry and was awarded the British War and Victory Medals. The Tamworth Herald published his obituary on 16th November 1918;

> *Cope.---On October 31st 1918, at 32 Stationary Hospital, France, of Influenza, Gunner William Ernest (R.G.A.), dearly-loved eldest son of Mr and Mrs Cope, The Green, Amington, in his 21st year. "Dearly loved and dearly mourned," from his loving father, mother, sisters, and brothers.*

(The War Gratuity mentioned was based on length of service giving a very rough estimate that he joined up between January and April 1917).

Chapter 7

Frank Daft

Frank was the youngest of three children born to James and Ellen Daft, in Nuneaton, October 1886. From available records, Frank did not have a good start in life, his mother died sometime between giving birth to him and the year 1891. In that year his father, James, a Labourer in a Wood Factory and still a widower, was resident at 17, Court 3, house 89, Abbey Street, Nuneaton. Frank's elder brother and sister were at school and it is not apparent who was looking after him while dad was at work. Perhaps there was family nearby or neighbours helped. By 1901, James Daft had passed away and Frank and his elder brother, Walter, are living at an address in Polesworth given as the Baptist Chapel, quite a few families also show this address on the census form so it is probably housing associated with the Chapel. The two boys are nephews of the head of house, William Stonehouse, whose family consists of his wife and six children, all in the same house. All the males of working age at the house are employed as miners in one job or another. Frank, at 14, is a Coupler, his job was to couple and uncouple the coal carrying carts, whilst his brother, Walter, was an underground Pony Driver. No doubt the boys became introduced to the mining industry at Pooley Hall Colliery following the death of their father by their Uncle, after moving to live with him and his family.

On 21st October 1909, Frank appeared before Mr Justice Pickman, charged with:

On or between 10th May and 31st July 1909 at the Parish of Nuneaton, feloniously did carnally know a girl Hilda Mary Wilson, a girl under the age of 13 years.

Frank pleaded guilty and the record shows he did not have previous convictions; he was sentenced to 10 months Hard Labour. Apart from the loss of liberty and the shame of his crime, the actual sentence would have involved hard manual work such as in a quarry or road building and not any harder than his normal work in the mine. A hard labour sentence could also have been served inside the prison, there were in some jails a Punishment Wheel, this device was just a large wheel which men could stand in and drive by walking. Sometimes the wheel had a functional purpose such as grinding corn and the prisoners could earn their keep, sometimes the wheel's sole function was punishment with no practical application.

In 1911, Frank was still resident with his uncle who had moved to 422, The Gullet, Polesworth, with his wife and two of his sons; both also miners. Frank was by now employed at Pooley Hall Colliery as a Filler and it would appear he had learned his lesson from his first brush with the law, as he never appeared in a court again.

Frank enlisted in the army at Atherstone in 1915 and although his military file has not survived, his medal card has and it shows that he was awarded the 1915 Star and his entitlement to this medal was dated 29th July 1915 and the theatre of war he entered on that date was France. The card also shows that Frank was initially inducted to the Leicester Regiment as Private 10782 and then transferred to 1st Battalion South Staffordshire Regiment as Private 32512.

Picture Author's Collection

It is likely that on attestation he was sent for basic training with the Leicester Regiment and then following successful completion of that, he was transferred to a Battalion in the field; this would give him a joining date in the Spring of 1915 and training with the 3rd Reserve Battalion, Leicester Regiment. The other option of course, was that he joined the Leicester Regiment earlier, possibly at the outbreak of war and opted to serve in Britain (which was an option at that time with a Territorial Battalion) and then in July 1915 volunteered for overseas service. Without his military file, we can never tell, but either way Frank did not wait for conscription to be implemented in 1916, he joined as a volunteer to serve his King and country.

On 29th July 1915, Frank landed in France and commenced his journey to join the 1st Battalion South Staffordshire Regiment in the field. The 1st Battalion had been stationed in South Africa at the outbreak of war and had been recalled to the UK landing at Southampton in September 1914. Following a short period of reorganisation and change of equipment, appropriate to Europe, the Battalion was sent to the continent landing at Zeebrugge,

Belgium, on October 14th 1914, Frank would have joined them during August 1915.

Towards the end of June 1916, the Battalion moved to shelters at a location named Grantown, they practised attack techniques in readiness for the 'Big Push' and, on 24th June, the heavy bombardment of the enemy trenches began. The shelters must have been near to the front line as casualties were being taken and on 28th June 1916, the attack they were waiting to participate in was postponed for a further 48 hours and the bombardment continued. This was very much a stressful time for the men as by this stage in the war they very well knew that an infantry attack would be met by well-placed machine gun nests delivering a lethal wall of lead, artillery and mortar fire. For one man it was too much and he self-inflicted a wound in an effort to get away from the front. It is a marvel to the bravery of the men that they could stand this anticipation and stress with courage, fortitude and self-discipline. On the day of the postponement, five men were wounded and one man died from wounds, presumably in the counter barrages sent over by the German artillery.

At 9.30 p.m. on 30th June 1916, the Battalion moved from the relative safety of the shelters to trenches in readiness for the attack. They spent the night in this location waiting for the whistle which would signify going over the top. At 7.30 a.m. 1st July 1916, the Battle of the Somme commenced and Frank and his comrades of the 1stBattalion, South Staffordshire Regiment climbed out of their trenches and attacked the German front line, their objective to capture the village of Mametz. By 9 a.m. the whole Battalion had entered the village with little resistance and casualties, but then one of the Companies encountered a large number of Germans in the south of the village and called for reinforcements. A Company of the 21st Manchester Regiment was despatched and by 11.20 a.m. the situation was under control and positions held being consolidated. There was still two final parts of the overall objective and fighting continued throughout the day and evening until this was achieved at 7.40 p.m. This first day of the battle was deemed a huge success for 1st South Staffordshire Regiment, 150 prisoners, two machine guns, automatic rifles, field telephones and large quantities of other stores had been taken, but success always has a cost and there were over 300 casualties killed and wounded. The night was quiet and the business of consolidating the positions was undertaken before the men rested, patrols and listening posts were sent out in front to warn of any counter attack. Over the next few days the attack was pressed forward and the Battalion moved forward to hold positions taken by other Battalions, artillery fire from the enemy continued to take a steady toll of casualties and on 5th July 1916 they were relieved under the protection of a heavy artillery bombardment.

The Battalion was placed in reserve until 14th July 1916 when it was again brought to the front to engage the enemy at High Wood, The movement to take up start positions was under heavy shellfire but by 6.30 p.m. they were in position and the attack was launched at 7 p.m. After only 100 yards the enemy were found to be holding shell holes and ground hollows forward of the objective and engaged them with rapid rifle fire and bombs. The infantry was assisted by a cavalry charge and two Royal Flying Corps aeroplanes made a huge difference strafing the German positions. About half of High Wood was taken but the other half was held with a fierce resistance and the men were ordered to hold their positions at all cost. It had become very difficult to get rations and water to the men but they held their ground despite the difficulties presented to them. Fighting continued all through the 15th July 1916 and, at 2.30 a.m. on 16th, the order was received to retire to a more defendable position. The movement was carried out under heavy fire and the men arrived back at Mametz at 5.30 a.m.

Casualties amounted to 18 killed, 143 wounded and 140 missing. The Battalion retired to the rear and went into rest camps where they enjoyed inter-Battalion football matches whilst they cleaned up, rested and received replacements.

During the evening of 29th August 1916, the Battalion moved into trenches East of Delville Wood and relieved 1st Royal Welsh Fusiliers (the correct spelling for this Regiment is Welch but during World War 1 they were referred to in this form, even the memorials are misspelt). The weather at this time was torrential rain and thunderstorms; the front line was a series of bomb craters joined together by trenches which were just filled with rivers of water and waist deep mud. Communications were not complete and runners were sent over the top, it would take them an hour to reach the front line through the mud, and ration parties took eight hours to deliver rations to the men. During the change over, the nearest dressing station was destroyed by shellfire. The rain continued throughout the following day as did the enemy artillery fire. During the day on 31st August, the enemy attacked the Battalion's positions with bombing parties, these attacks were repelled with bombs and sniping but as the day progressed the supply of bombs dwindled to a critical situation as very few supplies had managed to get through. At the start of this engagement the Battalion's strength was low at 18 officers and 700 other ranks but they now added ten officers wounded or missing (one RAMC Captain gassed), and 35 other ranks killed, 84 other ranks wounded and 146 other ranks missing. The Battalion was relieved at 6 a.m. on 1st September 1916, this was their last engagement during the Somme Offensive, their contribution great as was their sacrifice!

The rest of 1916 was spent on trench duty in a quiet sector of the front and apart from night time raids designed to blow in enemy Sap Heads and capture prisoners, the routine of front line, reserve and rest was a continuous cycle. Christmas 1916 was made special by the people of Walsall, the following diary entry for 20th December 1916 tells all:

In camp as above. Usual routine. The following letter was received from the Mayor of the Borough of Walsall:-
<u>*Christmas Gifts for Walsall Troops.*</u>
"The Committee at their meeting this afternoon decided to make a grant of £25:towards the entertainment of the men, and I beg to enclose a Bankers Draft for the amount. I shall be glad if you will kindly convey from me to the Officers and Men the best wishes of the inhabitants of this borough for Christmas and the New Year, and their appreciation of the efforts our brave soldiers are making for their King and Country."
This money was spent on the Christmas dinners.

Christmas day was spent in Kafir Camp, Bertrancourt and on Boxing Day they moved to billets at Mailly-Maillet. The return to trench duties occurred at 9 p.m., 10th January 1917, at Beaumont-Hamel where they prepared for action the following morning. Part of these preparations for entering the trenches was the distribution of gum boots and measures taken to protect the men's feet from Trench Foot, a condition caused by the long term immersion of the feet in water. Each man had to have three pairs of socks, his boots packed away in his pack and his feet rubbed in Whale Oil.

At 06.15 a.m., 11th January 1917, the Battalion formed up in preparation for the attack and an artillery bombardment commenced. The diary mentions 50 casualties occurring before the attack so presumably the German artillery replied and with the men concentrated in such a small area a few lucky shells must have hit the tightly grouped men. At 6.45 a.m., the attack commenced and the men moved forward in an orderly line, on reaching the German line the ground became extremely difficult to move over, many of the men becoming stuck in deep mud filled holes. The German trench was found to be obliterated and positions were created in shell holes, the day was spent consolidating the ground taken and creating strong points against counter attack. This work was constantly harassed by machine gun and sniper fire and the Battalion had to hold these positions all the following day until relieved at night. Casualties were; eight other ranks killed, five officers and 81 other ranks wounded, one officer and nine other ranks missing; searches to find the missing proved fruitless.

The following months of 1917 were a routine of trench relief, training and rest to the rear, during the time in the trenches a steady flow of casualties were reported mainly from artillery fire and the Battalion was involved in a few minor attacks, all of which Frank survived. At 3 p.m. on 3rd October 1917, Frank's Battalion relieved the Royal Welsh Fusiliers in the front line near to Hooge, Belgium, to take part in action conducted by the 2nd Army as part of the Third Battle of Ypres. At 4.30 a.m., 4thOctober, Frank and his Battalion comrades stepped up to the tape marking the starting point of their advance at a position east of Polygon Wood. Frank was equipped with his Lee Enfield Rifle, 220 rounds of .303 small arms ammunition (SAA), a haversack containing iron rations for one day, two sand bags, ground sheet rolled and containing a cardigan jacket, box respirator and P.H. helmet, bayonet and full water bottle. The iron rations were made up thus; 1 lb. preserved meat, 3 oz. cheese, 12 oz. biscuit, 5/8 oz. tea, 2 oz. sugar, 1/2 oz. salt, 1 oz. meat extract. The sandbags were to fill and use in the consolidation of any position taken, in particular if an enemy trench was taken, the fire step was now on the rear face and a new step had to be made immediately for the troops to fire from in the event of a counter attack.

Forming up for the attack had started at 1 a.m. and throughout the process there was heavy shelling from the enemy artillery.

The attack commenced at 6 a.m. and the Battalion started moving towards the German positions, resistance was not very heavy but many German soldiers were shot or bayoneted and a number of pill boxes had to be dealt with. Machine gun fire on the right flank caused some casualties but the Battalion reached its initial objective and allowed the next Battalion in line to continue through their ranks and press the attack, Frank and his comrades went about the business of consolidating the positions they occupied. At 1 p.m., the enemy opened up with medium and light artillery and this continued throughout the afternoon and evening. The night went quietly, but in the morning machine gun fire and sniping caused numerous casualties. The Battalion held its positions throughout the day and in the afternoon suffered heavy shelling which continued through the night of the 5th October 1914. It was during this period that Frank became a casualty to the artillery and like many other men, his body was never recovered. The 8th Devonshire Regiment finally relieved the 1st Staffordshire Regiment during the night of 6th October 1914, the recorded losses to the Battalion were; three officers and 36 other ranks killed, seven officers and 323 other ranks wounded, 49 other ranks missing which included Frank but he was later reported killed in action. To balance this terrible loss the Battalion's gains were; an advance of 800-900 yards on a front of 450 yards, an estimated 150 enemy soldiers killed, 80-100 Germans taken prisoner and sent to the rear as POW's, six light machine guns and six medium trench mortars captured.

Frank left £33.2s.4d. to a Mr George Mundy and this account was settled in 1920, he was of course awarded the 1914-15 star, British War and Victory medals. Frank's name is engraved on the Memorial Wall of Tyne Cot Cemetery, West-Vlaanderen, Belgium. This cemetery is the largest British and Commonwealth cemetery in the world with 11,954 men buried there. The memorial was constructed to honour the names of 34,959 men with no known grave who fell after 15th August 1917 as the intended memorial for all those missing in the Ypres Salient, Menin Gate, was found not to be big enough. In total, there were five battles for Ypres and by 1918, this once beautiful City had been reduced to rubble. It was at Ypres in 1914 that the British Expeditionary Force had halted the German advance through Belgium, but the German forces surrounded the city on three sides and pounded it with artillery from the high points which they held. The high cost to the British and French armies was their advances from the Ypres Salient into the surrounding hills to dislodge the German forces from their advantageous positions. Frank was one of between an estimated 800,000 to 1.2 million casualties during the five battles for the city of Ypres.

Chapter 8

William Dean

In 1888, Albert and Jane Dean started their family with the birth of a son, William. The birth was registered as occurring in the 4th quarter of that year in Tamworth, Staffordshire. Two years later in 1891, the family, now resident at 6, Alvecote Cottages, Shuttington, Tamworth, had been added to with a second child, a daughter. Living with them was a brother-in-law of Albert's, William Moseley, who was also a Coal Miner. Coincidentally, living a few doors away at number 3, Alvecote Cottages, was the Harper family which included Thomas Harper who is also commemorated on the Pooley Hall Memorial. By 1901, the family now resident at 13, Peel Street, Tamworth, had been expanded to six children; the youngest being Charles aged three months. William at 12 is not shown as employed or as a scholar and his father was now employed as a bricklayer.

Between 1901 and 1911, William was employed at the Pooley Hall Colliery and joined the army. In the 1911 Census he is shown as resident at South Barracks Gibraltar and serving with 1st Battalion, South Staffordshire Regiment. William's military file does not exist and it is impossible to say whether he was serving with the Regiment at the outbreak of World War I or whether he had left and was subject to immediate recall. What is certain is that he mobilised to France at the same time as the 2nd Battalion South Staffordshire Regiment.

On 4th August 1914, the Commanding Officer of 2nd Battalion, stationed at Aldershot, received orders to mobilise immediately for France. Within two days they were ready and entrained to Southampton on 12th August where they embarked on SS Irrawaddy, disembarking at Le Havre France. After a day at No 1 Camp, the Battalion received orders which resulted in daily route marches until 24th August when they arrived at Harmingies where they were assigned the task of covering the retreat being made by the Division in the face of the German offensive. They formed a defensive position in the Village of Bauay and waited for the German spearhead to arrive, when it did there was little fighting and the Battalion followed the Division and retired behind it forming defensive rear-guard actions as they retired. William's experience now follows that of his Battalion and Pooley Hall colleague Arthur Jackson; Arthur was killed in action on 10th March 1915.

At an unknown point from this date, William was transferred back to the 1st Battalion South Staffordshire Regiment. Without his file it is impossible to say when, but it is very likely that at the time of mobilisation William was a reservist and on recall mobilised with the 2nd Battalion rather than wait until the 1st returned to England from South Africa. There is a discrepancy with his medal records, some of which show him as 2nd Battalion, but what is certain, is that he entered France on the same date as 2nd Battalion and was killed in action on 25th September 1915. On this date the 2nd Battalion's diary records only wounded casualties, no killed and no missing, whilst 1st Battalion were in action for several days and records fierce fighting with casualties of all categories, the Commonwealth War Graves Commission also record his Battalion as the 1st.

Between 9th and 13th September 1915, 1st Battalion were in front line trenches at Noyelles. It was a quiet period spent holding the line in the day and working parties at night to improve the trenches. Only two men were wounded, one of whom died of his wounds on 13th, the day the Battalion was relieved and went to the rear to clean, rest, take baths and train in assault tactics. On 23rd September, the men returned to reserve trenches at Noyelles. At 9.30 p.m., the following day, they moved to front line trenches in preparation for an attack on the German lines as part of the Battle of Loos. It was raining very hard and the men spent the night cold and wet in anticipation of the attack to come. During 24th September, the rain continued and the trenches were half full of water, at 10 p.m., they moved to start positions where they spent the night in knee-deep mud and continuous rain.

The Battalion's objective for the forthcoming attack was a 450 yard wide, German front line. It was fortified with flank defences, exceptionally thick wire to its front, numerous small redoubts containing many machineguns and was also protected by fire from Hohenzollern Fort and Fosse 8 (a fortified coal slag heap). The British front line was 300 yards in length and manned by C Company under the command of Lieutenant William Cooper who would lead the attack. C Company comprised; 138 riflemen, 19 machine gunners, 21 grenade men, two stretcher bearers and four signallers, totalling 184 men. A and D Companies were similarly manned and in support trenches with B Company in reserve. It is useful to note that these three supporting Companies fielded a greater number of stretcher bearers with B Company having eight.

At 6.28 a.m. on 25th September 1915, the order, "Get ready to Charge" came down the line and Lieutenant Cooper gave the order, "Scouts and wire cutters advance" and so the Company climbed the ladders over the parapet and commenced the 500 yards' advance to their objective. The advance was protected by a dense fog caused by smoke bombs, candles and British gas, there was also a continuous drizzle of rain and a cold mist. A Company followed on and then D Company, casualties started almost immediately and both officers leading C and A

Companies died on the German wire. Despite terrible casualties caused by heavy enemy machine gun and rifle fire, the attack was pressed and the German line taken to the second support line. There then commenced a six day battle where the German forces counter attacked to dislodge the British from their captured positions. The Battalion was not relieved until 3 a.m. on 30th September 1915 when they retired to billets at Sailly La Bourse.

Throughout the battle, it had continued to rain heavily and many of the bodies unrecovered were either destroyed by explosions or slipped into the mud and could well be still in the ground where they fell. The casualty list for this period is; 18 officers and 430 other ranks killed or wounded, this is out of 21 officers and 729 other ranks who went into battle on 25th September 1915. William was one of the men killed in this action and his body was never identified or recovered.

William left £16.1s.0d supplemented by a War Gratuity of £4 to his father Albert. He was awarded the 1914 Star, British War and Victory Medals and his name was engraved on the Loos memorial panel, 73 to 76.

Chapter 9

Thomas Henry Frost

Princess Mary Gift Tin (Photo Courtesy Mr T Thurlow)

Thomas Frost has the singular coincidence of being the first man wounded in the Battalion he went to war with and then wounded again in the last action of the Battalion he was serving with at the end of the war.

Thomas was born in Wilnecote, Tamworth on 24th February 1989. His parents, Arthur and Emily Frost, lived on Belgrave Road and had five older children. Arthur Frost was a coal miner working as a Stallman. Aged 12, Thomas left school and sought employment as a Brickyard labourer. He later followed his father into the industry and was initially employed as a Coal Miner Roadman at Birch Coppice Colliery, Polesworth where he worked for six years prior to enlistment in the army. On 23rd March 1913, Thomas married Mary Alice Barker at St Andrews Church, Bordesley, Birmingham.

On 5th November 1914, Thomas attended one of the Birmingham recruitment facilities and following his medical examination and attestation was posted to the King's Royal Rifle Corps (KRRC) 9th (Service) Battalion, C Company, as Rifleman R6577. The medical report shows that Thomas was tall for a miner and man of his day at 5'7½" tall, weighing 133 lbs. He reported on 10th November 1914, to the 9th Battalion, KRRC which was formed in August 1914 at Winchester. The Battalion then moved to Aldershot, Grayshott and Bordon Camps, before moving back to Aldershot in February 1915. During this time the Battalion trained and equipped itself for war. On May 11th 1915, the Battalion received its mobilisation orders. There followed days of frenzied activity to gather all the men, their equipment, transport, stores, horses and, with the assistance of three trains, the Battalion was taken to Southampton and Folkestone. The first party embarked from Southampton and landed at Le Havre on 20th May 1915, the second and third trainloads embarked from Folkestone aboard the SS Victoria, landing at Boulogne on 21st May 1915. The Battalion was reunited at a rest camp where, on May 21st, they paraded for the first time on foreign soil; 29 officers and 841 men lined up to hear the King's message following which three cheers for His Majesty were voiced. That afternoon the men were entertained in the YMCA hut by Lena Ashwell and her concert party, along with the sunny weather the war hadn't been too bad so far.

The following day, 22nd May 1915, the Battalion entrained and marched to Cassel, from here they could hear the distant guns of the front line. Despite the hot weather the next few days were spent marching by Company, inspecting some example trenches receiving tuition in their construction and maintenance. There being no better training in trench warfare than actual front line experience, the men were moved nearer to the front line and at each stopping point further training was given in the use of respirators and changing magazines. By 31st May, the Battalion were billeted at Canada Huts, Dickesbuche and from here they went out at night to dig reserve trenches on the Yser Canal, 1½ miles South of Ypres. It was here that the men experienced their first hostile fire when they came under fire from German machine guns.

This work continued into the first few days of June and then on 6th June 1915, the Battalion was split to different locations to enter the front line for the first time and receive training in trench warfare. C and D Companies were sent to trenches at Saint-Éloi to join the King's Own Yorkshire Light Infantry (KOYLI) and Queens Own Royal West Kent regiments. On the way to these trenches, Thomas was hit in the left leg by a bullet and evacuated to an aid station and became the first battle casualty of the 9th Battalion KRRC. Following treatment at a dressing station, Thomas was taken to hospital and from there evacuated back to England and admitted to 3rd London General Hospital in Wandsworth on 10th June 1915. Thomas was only in hospital for six days as the wound had healed, X-Rays showed that he had suffered an incomplete fracture of the Fibular (Lower leg) and the injury would probably not leave permanent damage, he was discharged. Following a period of rehabilitation, Thomas was posted to the 5th (Reserve) Battalion based at Sheerness, where he remained classified as unfit for further Foreign Service.

Thomas had several run-ins with military discipline whilst posted with the 5th Battalion. Foran offence of improper conduct on parade, he was awarded extra fatigues; and being late on sick

parade, three days confined to barracks. For three offences of overstaying a leave pass, he was again confined to barracks for three days and on one occasion ordered to forfeit three day's pay.

During a period of leave at home, Thomas had been to see his old employers, Morris and Shaw Ltd, Birch Coppice Colliery. As a result, the Colliery manager wrote to the Commanding officer of 5th Battalion on 5th December 1916, requesting that Thomas be released from military service to resume his employment at the Colliery. Thomas was discharged from the army on 11th December 1916 and transferred to Class W of the army reserve and resumed his employment at Birch Coppice Colliery as a Miner and Getter. This status was subject to review and on 3rd May 1917, Thomas declared that he was working in the above capacity at Birch Coppice whilst answering a form sent to him that also requested details of his 'approved society', Thomas declared that he was a member of the Order of Druids. (A fraternal order formed in 1781 in London, constructed on a Lodge basis. Winston Churchill was a member of Albion Lodge in Oxford).

On 12th April 1918, Thomas attended Brocton Camp, Stafford as part of his commitment as a reservist and the following day was subjected to a medical examination where he was re-categorised "A" by the Travelling Medical Board (TMB). Category A, meant that Thomas was fit for General Service in that he could march, see to shoot, hear well and stand active service conditions. Whilst the medical noted the scar on his left leg, his original medical assessment that the wound would not be a permanent disability now meant that the shortage of man power took precedence over his physical condition and important work as a miner. Even the fact that Thomas had few or no teeth was overcome by fitting him with a denture plate, he was posted back to 5th (Reserve) Battalion and from there to the 13th Battalion who were serving on the Western Front, arriving there in the field on 22nd June 1918.

The 13th Battalion KRRC was stationed between Arras and Albert in the Somme region at this time and had been fighting on the northern edge of the primary offensive line of the German Spring Offensive. By the time that Thomas joined the fight, the situation had stabilised and the German advance held. On 8th August, the Allied Armies launched a counter attack from Amiens in France, to Mons in Belgium known as the Hundred Days Offensive. Following the failure of Germany's Spring Offensive, they now held ground of dubious value and were having difficulty maintaining supplies to the front-line units, the Allied Offensive was designed to push the German army out of France.

Thomas's short war experience in 1915 was so short that he had not even reached a front-line trench when he was shot. The position of the wound in his lower left leg would suggest that they were approaching the front line above ground. By now the trench system had become much more sophisticated with a three-tier system of reserve, support and front line, all inter-connected by communication trenches both open and covered. The equipment the men were issued with was much improved, such as effective gas masks and hoods and the greatest of all innovations, the tank. Whilst the static nature of World War I was created by the scientific placement and use of machineguns, the tank was the invention to break this deadlock. Another innovation which was present in 1915, but by now in much greater quantity, was the aeroplane. On 1st April 1918, the Royal Flying Corps and the Royal Naval Air Service were amalgamated to become the Royal Air Force and now formed the third arm of the British forces. It was by now, a far more common sight to see aerial battles in the skies over the trenches as well as their use as artillery spotters.

During August 1918, the 13th Battalion held front line trenches on a rotation basis, but on 25th August orders were received that the Battalion would take part in an attack on the village of Favreuil that night. At 5 p.m., the Companies were in their start positions and began to move forward to assembly points. During this movement, the men were subjected to heavy artillery, machinegun fire and nine enemy aircraft flying over, firing at the advancing troops. At 6.36 p.m., with all men in position, the Allied artillery bombardment commenced on the German positions to be attacked, the target points were 700 yards to the front and a quick advance was made to catch up with the artillery. All Companies pressed on with the attack in the face of heavy machinegun fire and by 7.15 p.m. 73 German prisoners were being brought to the rear, they reported that the target village was occupied by a whole Regiment that had come forward the previous night, despite this the attack was continued. The Battalion was fighting in this engagement until 3 a.m. on 26th August 1918 when it was relieved and retired to rest in Logeast Wood. By now the target village was partly taken and German forces in front had surrendered. The casualty figures for the month largely reflect the loss sustained during this engagement; six officers and 39 other ranks killed, 11 officers and 279 other ranks wounded, 32 other ranks missing. In addition to six German officers and 535 other ranks taken prisoner, also captured were 38 machineguns, four trench mortars with two hand carts and a box of spare parts, two anti-tank rifles, two field guns and a horse with saddle and bridle.

The rest of August 1918 was spent in camp in Logeast Wood engaged in salvage work and practising Battalion attack. On 3rd September, the Battalion moved back to Favreuil where they made camp and went into Divisional reserve. The time here was spent training and providing working parties for salvage operations; large quantities of equipment both German and British were recovered and taken to the Divisional salvage dump.

On 12th September 1918, the Battalion again went into the fore of the offensive with orders to attack the village of Trescault. At 5.25 a.m. that morning, the Battalion began its attack under the cover of a very effective artillery barrage. Despite heavy resistance throughout the day with the Battalion experiencing casualties from shell, machinegun and rifle fire, the day was successful with 190 prisoners, 118 machineguns, three trench mortars, one anti-tank gun and two field guns being captured. Apart from the usual retaliatory measures, the Germans also fired a large quantity of blue and yellow cross gas shells, this was a particularly nasty use of gas in warfare in that the first shells fired were marked with a blue cross and dispersed a very fine particle irritant, which was designed to penetrate the filters of the British gas mask causing uncontrollable sneezing and coughing, forcing the wearer to remove the mask. The second shell fired was marked with a yellow cross and contained a lethal gas designed to kill the men who had been forced to remove their masks, this was known as Mustard Gas due to the smell and apart from causing severe damage to the lungs it also had a blistering effect on exposed skin. This tactic had been first used in 1917 and fortunately the British developed a filter to contain the fine particle gas thereby making the tactic ineffective, however, Mustard gas did not disperse quickly and its use made the area poisonous for days afterwards.

Following this engagement, the Battalion went into a support line and then reserve where they again formed working parties and trained. This pattern continued for the rest of September and throughout October 1918, from support positions they would push through the front line and press the attack on small objectives. Casualties were sustained in a steady flow from the usual causes, prisoners and enemy equipment captured during each attack, the 100-day offensive was proving successful. At the end of October, the Battalion's strength had been reduced from 915 to 800, but they had gained an officer the establishment of which was 40. The losses included two officers and

25 other ranks killed, seven officers and 132 other ranks wounded, ten other ranks gas casualties and one underage soldier was discovered and returned to base.

At 3.30 a.m. on 4th November 1918, the 13th Battalion again formed up at assembly positions to resume their role in the offensive, their objective was to capture the village of Louvignies. Three tanks had been assigned to follow the Battalion but they did not show, clearly the tactics of tanks being supported by Infantry, successfully used during the Second World War had not yet been developed and a tank following Infantry could not be used unless called forward to deal with a strong point. The enemy were alert to the coming attack and opened a heavy artillery barrage on the assembly positions between 4 and 5 a.m. At 05.30 a.m., the whistles sounded and the men commenced their attack behind the cover of an artillery bombardment. German machinegun positions had been established in the orchards and hedges around the target village and an effective enfilade was experienced by the Battalion's leading companies. These positions were targeted and many Germans killed, bitter hand to hand fighting ensued and many of the enemy casualties were caused by bayonet thrusts. In one instance an NCO found himself in a cellar with three Germans, the diary gives a feel for the vicious nature of the fight;

> *'Heavy machinegun fire was opened from the orchards and hedges around the village but the attack was strongly pushed and the enemy severely handled.*
>
> *In many cases, as soon as our men were within hand-to-hand fighting distance, the enemy surrendered, but here and there more determined resistance was met with and considerable bayonet work took place. On the right front C Coy about 70 dead Germans were counted.*
>
> *The field ambulance informed our MO that an unusually large number of enemy wounded passed through suffering from severe bayonet wounds.*

Several gory individual contests took place in cellars. One NCO of B Coy fought with 3 Huns in a cellar and killed the lot. His weapon was a small hand axe which he was carrying to cut his way through hedges, and so the good work went on.'

During the morning, Thomas had become a victim of the enemy machine guns positioned around the village, he was hit in the arms and legs and taken to the aid station and then to one of four Casualty Clearing Stations based near to the village of Caudry. Thomas did not recover from his injuries. He died on 7th November 1918 and was buried in the British Cemetery there. Thomas's cause of death is not recorded and could have been from several reasons, such as shock from trauma or blood loss, but the fact he lasted as long as he did would indicate a more common reason, Sepsis. When a bullet enters the body, it pushes before it all it meets and this includes clothing, shreds of Thomas's mud covered uniform would have been pushed by the bullets into the wounds that they caused and become a source of infection within the wound which would develop into Sepsis. Without the benefit of anti-biotics, the medical professionals had little to fight the onset of this poisoning which would spread rapidly and kill the victim often within a few days, the time scale would support this synopsis.

Documentation which has survived as part of his file show that his widow, Mary, who was now living with her father in law at 328, Wilnecote Lane, Belgrave, Tamworth, received a pension of 13 shillings and 9 pence per week from May 1919. She also received his medals, the 1914-15 Star, Victory and British War Medals, plus the Princess Mary gift given to all service personnel who were serving at Christmas 1914.

Chapter 10

Thomas Harper

Thomas Harper was born in 1876 in Bilston, Staffordshire, to Thomas and Rosannah Harper. In 1881 the family were living at Moors Yard, Wilnecote, Tamworth. Thomas (junior) was the third child but the only boy of five children. All were born in Bilston, except for the youngest who for some reason was Welsh having arrived into the world at Wrexham. By 1891 Thomas (senior) had moved his family to 3, Alvecote Cottages, Shuttington, Tamworth, there were now seven children, two more boys having been born. Rosannah had the benefit of live-in help in the form of 17 year old Susannah Bennett, a young lady from Kings Heath Birmingham who was employed as a Maid. It appears that the children were leaving school at 12, as Thomas (Junior) was also employed as a Coal Miner, his 14 year old sister was a domestic servant and the next youngest child at age 11 was still a scholar.

In 1895 Thomas joined the Tamworth Volunteers. These local volunteer units were aligned to a local regiment and subsequently formed the Territorial Units of the British Army. On 16th January 1900, Thomas (Junior) attended Whittington Barracks, Lichfield, the home of the North Staffordshire (Prince of Wales) Regiment, where he was subjected to a medical examination and attested to join the army. On this date he also declared that he was currently serving as a member of 2nd Battalion North Staffordshire Regiment and this is probably a reference to his service with the

Tamworth Volunteers. Private 7141 Harper, standing 5'6¼ weighing 147 lbs of fair complexion and light brown hair, was judged fit for military service and commenced basic training. On 2nd March 1900, Thomas was sent to South Africa to join 2nd Battalion, who served throughout the Boer War from 1899-1902. On 1st April 1901, Thomas was discharged from the army, whilst in South Africa, where he remained for an unknown period as part of the Commander in Chief's bodyguard; he was paid a War Gratuity of £5 on discharge, for his part in the Boer War.

By October 1902, Thomas had returned to England, he was living in Glascote, Tamworth and had resumed his career as a Coal Miner. On 20th October, he married Clara Padbury at St Paul's Church, Warwick. Clara was the same age as Thomas, 27, and was from Earl Shilton, Leicestershire. They commenced a family two years later and by 1911 had three children and were living at The Elms, Glascote, Tamworth, a five roomed house. Thomas was now employed as a Hewer at the Pooley Hall Colliery, when war broke out he returned to the Colours and re-joined the North Staffordshire Regiment at a Tamworth recruiting facility. Private 292 Harper was posted to the 1/6th Battalion which had been formed at Burton-On-Trent in August 1914 and was then moved to a Camp at Bishops Stortford.

On 5th March 1915, the Battalion mobilised to France landing at Le Havre the following day, 6th March 1915. Thomas's file from this stage of his military service, did not survive the bombing of the Blitz in World War II, but what is known was that his experience as a Soldier and Miner elevated him very quickly to the rank of Sergeant, attached to the newly formed Tunnelling Companies working under the guidance of the Royal Engineers. Thomas's story is recorded in the reports and citations concerning the rescue attempts made after he became a casualty whilst working for the 172nd Tunnelling Company, which was formed on 1st April 1915 and was working in the Bluff/St Eloi areas at Ypres Belgium. On 27th April 1915, Thomas was part of an underground working party who had descended into a tunnel where a mine had been exploded to destroy German Mining operations and of course kill as many of the enemy in the process. Poisonous fumes overcame the men and a rescue attempt mounted. Unfortunately Thomas died in the tunnel; it was believed he had choked to death whilst lying on his back and his false teeth had assisted the choking process. Nine of the men involved in the rescue were recommended for, and subsequently received, the Distinguished Conduct Medal. Three of these men served with the Tamworth Volunteers; Privates Rowland Hill, Arthur Storer and Albert Thomas Weston. These men, together with four other Tamworth Territorials, sent a letter about Thomas's death which was published in the Herald on May 8, 1915:

"I regret to say that Sergeant T Harper No 292 was killed in action on Tuesday night, April 27. He is mourned by us as a big friend. We were all attached to him, for he proved himself a man. We gave him a fitting funeral, and as we are billeted close by, his grave will have every attention it needs. We extend our deepest sympathy to his wife and children in their sad loss. Yours sincerely, Sappers R Hill, AT Weston, T West, A Storer, W Cockerham, J Detheridge – Sgt Harper belonged to Glascote."

Thomas's body was recovered and he was buried in Kemmel Chateau Military Cemetery, Belgium. He left £8.0s.11d, supplemented by a War Gratuity of £6, to his wife Clara who also received his 1914-15 Star, British War and Victory Medals, plus a war widows pension of amount unknown.

Chapter 11

James Hennessey

James is rather an unusual case as he was not a local man, nor did he come from a background of coal mining. His connection with the Polesworth area is unknown but from a newspaper article announcing his death we know that prior to the start of World War I, he was resident at Thomas Street, Glascote, Tamworth, and had been working at Pooley Hall Colliery.

James was born on 22nd January 1891 in Baltinglass, Kildare, County Wicklow Ireland. His parents were William and Kate (*nee* Rooney) Hennessey who lived at Chapel Hill, Baltinglass. As was the custom with Catholic families, James was baptised on the first available date, 1st March 1891. The census of 1901, filled in by the local Constable James Peters, shows that the Hennessey family consisted of father who was a General Labourer, mother and nine children, ages ranging from under one to 18. James at ten years old, was a schoolboy and fifth eldest child. The two children older than 14 were in employment and with three incomes into the household Kate could afford to employ a live-in servant. Mary Kinsella was a 12-year-old girl who was a scholar but employed as a child nurse. All members of the household were educated to a read and write standard, with the exception of the youngest member and all were English speaking.

There is no sign of James in either England or Ireland at the time of the 1911 Census and perhaps he was travelling to his new career in the coal mines of Tamworth. It would appear that James joined the army in Tamworth at the outbreak of war and was posted to the 1st Battalion of the Irish Guards as Guardsman 5054. The Battalion had been mobilised from their base in Wellington Barracks eight days after war was declared and landed at Le Havre on 13th August 1914 as part of the 4th Guards Brigade of the 2nd Division. Whatever James's basic training consisted of, he was sent out to join the Battalion in France before Christmas but after 22nd November 1914. We can tell this by the fact that he was awarded the 1915 Star and eligibility for this medal ceased at this latter date and his newspaper obituary states that he had joined his unit in France before Christmas. It is also possible that he had previously served with the Irish Guards and at the start of the war was a reservist whose call up did not occur immediately. Without his military file we have no way of knowing.

The haste with which James was sent to the front was no doubt due to the devastating losses of the 1st Battalion during the course of the first stages of the war. They were engaged in the Battle of Mons and the subsequent retreat, the Battle of Marne, the Battle of the Aisne and the First Battle of Ypres. By the end of this last conflict, on 22nd November, the Battalion had suffered over 700casualties. Considering that the Battalion's strength on arriving in France was 997, these losses were enormous.

The next major engagement that the 1st Battalion was engaged in was the Battle of Loos which started on the 25th September and ended on 13th October 1915. On 9th August 1915, James succumbed to wounds he had received on a previous date and died. Due to the lack of battle action at this time it is probable that James's wounds occurred during a period holding the line from artillery or sniper fire, the vast majority of trench wounds occurring whilst in the front line were from shrapnel caused by artillery shells. It is also likely, from where he was buried, that he died in the dressing station that was in a house also used as Battalion HQ, at a crossroads known as Windy Corner near to the village of Cuinchy. Windy Corner was so called as it was a five way road junction where all traffic of one form or another passed through, the windy related to the emotion rather than the weather and probably because the junction was a continuous target of enemy artillery and 'it got a bit windy going through there'.

James was buried in grave 1.A.14 of the cemetery serving the dressing station, which later became known as Guards Cemetery, Windy Corner. The record of soldiers effects shows that James left, £3.3s.3d which was supplemented by a War Gratuity of £3 to his mother Kate. The one document from his military file which has survived, because it was sent to the records office in Ireland and not destroyed in the Blitz, is James' last will and testament, where he named his mother a sole legatee.

Photo from author's collection.

James was awarded the 1914-15 Star, British War and Victory medals.

Chapter 12

Zachariah Hedges

In 1885 in New Invention, Staffordshire, Margaret Hedges gave birth to a baby boy. This was her third child and the parents named him Zachariah. Zachariah's father, Frederick, was a Joiner by profession and in 1891 the family were living at New Hampton Road, New Invention. One more child had been added after Zachariah and they now had Margaret's mother living with them. By 1901 the family were now resident at Stowheath Lane, Willenhall, Staffordshire and consisted of the four eldest children plus a 17 year old lodger who worked in the mining industry as an above ground Engine Driver. Zachariah, aged 14, was employed as an Oddwork Stamper (likely to be related to Steelworks someone who pushes ore) and may have been influenced by the boarder to seek employment in the coal industry as he worked at Pooley Hall Colliery for some years prior to World War 1. In 1907 he married Lucy Rowley in Wolverhampton and by 1911 the couple had two sons and were living at 21, John Street, Nuneaton. Zachariah was employed as a Bond Minder at Pooley Hall.

At the outbreak of war, Zachariah, a member of the army reserve, immediately enlisted at Nuneaton to join the Royal Warwickshire Regiment. Private 11914 Hedges was posted to 11th (Service) Battalion which was formed at Warwick in September 1914. Zachariah was sent to Ludderhall on Salisbury Plain where the Battalion had been allocated tented accommodation at Windmill Hill Camp. Things were a little chaotic at this time as most of the men and officers had not seen previous service. Training was commenced but not structured in a traditional way and discipline was not being kept to a required standard. A large problem at this early stage was men going absent without leave or returning late from authorised leave.

In March 1915, the command of the Battalion now only five months old, was passed to Lieutenant Colonel C.S. Collison, who on arrival took up residency in one of the better hotels on Brighton's seafront. Collinson was a professional soldier who had retired in 1911 but had commanded a reserve Battalion for the previous three years.

At this stage the Battalion's strength was 1000 other ranks and 100 officers, but very few men had any previous military experience, even fewer possessed uniform or rifles most of the men were dressed in a blue outfit made of serge usually referred to as Kitchener Blues and sourced from old Post Office stock, this was a temporary issue until sufficient Khaki kit could be made and distributed. (The numbers given are from Colonel Collison's memoirs and are undoubtedly accurate but reflect the disorganisation of the situation). 100 officers is a huge number and was probably because men were waiting to be posted. On the plus side, the general morale was excellent, the men being enthusiastic and in a good state of health and fitness. Many of the officers had no idea of training and whilst they had taken part in divisional training, the basics at platoon and company level had been neglected. Collinson immediately commenced a programme of training from scratch and this progressed very quickly due to the enthusiasm of all concerned.

In April 1915, following a month of intensive training, the Battalion was moved from Shoreham to Ludgershall on Salisbury Plain where they formed the 4thBattalion of the 112th brigade under the command of Brigadier-General J. Marriott, D.S.O., M.V.O. The situation with regards to uniform and equipment was improving and by the end of May things were complete; the 11th now looked and behaved like a professional unit of the British army.

Training continued concluding with divisional operations and an inspection by the King on 25thJune, preparatory to embarkation to the front.

On 29th June, the Battalion's strength was swollen by 200, all other ranks, but men returning to active service from sickness and wounds. These were men who had already experienced war and the awful conditions beyond the comprehension of virgin soldiers, but they were to prove a huge asset in the days to come.

On 30th July 1915, at 01.30 hours, the advance party entrained at Ludgershall with over 70 animals, mainly mules, in a very efficient 42 minutes; the mules were surely playing the game! Embarkation from Folkestone to Le Havre was the destination for this first group. The next two groups followed at 15.30 and 16.30 on 31st July, but disembarked at Boulogne. The Battalion regrouped after 36 hours at Pont de Brique and took a train to Audruicq arriving at 3.30 p.m. on 1st August. The journey to the front then commenced with a short march to Zutkerque where the men were billeted around the village. It was from this point, although well away from the front, that Zachariah first heard war away to the north east, artillery gunfire. The journey to the front continued by marching from day to day in hot dry dusty conditions along roads designed for the carriage of people and goods on a much smaller scale than 1000 men marching, plus pack animals, carts full of everything from cooking utensils to ordnance. At 14.00 on 5th August, the primary objective of Hazebrouck, (13-15 miles from the front line), was reached and the men distributed to billets in a partly built, dirty, disused hospital complex. The diary records that 25 men 'fell out' during this arduous march, but the Brigadier was pleased at the appearance of the Battalion as it marched into town.

The enemy were active in this area, a recent attack on trenches in the region had been successful largely due to the use of 'liquid fire'for the first time against British troops, or as we now know the devices, flame throwers. The German air force, *Die Fliegertruppe*or Imperial German Air Service was also active dropping bombs from the air. Fortunately at this stage, the art of aerial bombardment was in its infancy and extremely inaccurate.

Zachariah's first visit to the front was on 10th August 1915 when a detachment marched 13 miles for trench digging work at Lorre which was the headquarters of the 28th Division. On arrival that evening they were welcomed by the Germans who fired two artillery shells which landed nearby. The event was marked with excited cheers, no one was hurt but this wasn't to last. Working with regular bombardments from enemy artillery would eventually bring a successful result and on 20th August the Battalion experienced its first casualty when Private 8744 Richards was severely injured by a shrapnel bullet in the right shoulder. It is interesting to note that early entries in war diaries often mention early casualties by name but as time goes on and the casualties pile up the personal touch is replaced by a note of numbers killed, wounded or missing, separately noting officers and other ranks.

Whilst Zachariah and his comrades dug, the rest of the Battalion - still 13 miles to their rear - practised 'musketry'. A rifle range had been constructed and the bill for its construction is recorded at ten Francs and 15 Centimes, just over £1!

The two parts of the Battalion were reunited on 24th August1915. The total strength was now recorded as 28 officers and 990 other ranks. The following day they entrained in open cattle trucks for a journey south arriving at Doullens at 2 a.m. on the 26th. They were met by 'English ladies' who supplied each man with hot cocoa, I am sure this greeting was a huge boost to the men's moral and the ladies probably received many offers of marriage that night! The men were then marched to Amplier arriving at 04.30. The day was spent receiving instruction in trench warfare. The march to the front continued the following day and on arrival at Sailly-au-bois as night fell, the Battalion by company and platoon were guided to reserve positions in the village of Hebuterne. The following week was spent learning the intricacies of the trench system, where the relevant positions were, the support and communication trenches, dug outs, location of stores and ammunition. Without this foresight, it would have been very easy to become lost in the maze of trenches.

Hebuterne was typical of front line villages and towns, largely destroyed by artillery bombardment. The church had received-serious attention as did other identifiable buildings such as hospitals, which the enemy sought to destroy as they were a focal point for potential victims and of course to diminish the moral of those who would value such facilities. A large crucifix with an effigy of Jesus stood proud in the churchyard and had been untouched. Those with religious leanings could take solace from this apparent miracle. Zachariah lived in the support trenches which was safer than having a roof over his head in the village. During this period, he was entertained to the aerial display of a dog fight between British and German airmen, the fascination of this spectacle was never diminished by familiarity.

During the night of 2nd September 1915, the 11th took their places in the front for the first time. These changeovers were always undertaken at night, in darkness and silence, to avoid bringing the manoeuvre to the attention of German gunners, a well-placed shell in a communication trench would create many casualties. The men of the 11th were now the closest they had ever been to enemy troops, along their section of line the distance to the German front line varied from 250 to 800 yards. This night was the last practical exercise of the trench warfare training; again comment is made about the enthusiasm and professional approach by all ranks.

At 7p.m. on 4th September 1915, the 11th left these positions and commenced a march to Humbercamps, arriving their early on the 5th and were allocated to billets, barns and outhouses for the men; the officers roomed in the village but had to share four beds.

Another move was commenced on 8th September a few miles back in the direction of the enemy lines at Berles-au-Bois where a dirty and dangerous job awaited them. The landscape in this part of France differs very much to the flat fields of Flanders where the 11th were first stationed, here there are rolling hill features and the job was to dig a new communication on a hillside but facing the enemy! The work could only be conducted at night and a line had been laid for the diggers to crawl out to from the safety of trenches, the exposed length was about 300 yards. On the first night, an attempt was made to cover the men's work with fire from the front line. Unfortunately, this drew attention to the situation and fire was returned with flares being used to illuminate the sky. The second night the work was conducted without covering fire and with the diggers gradually moving deeper the work became safer. It's rather remarkable that there were no casualties during this operation especially on the first night where the retaliatory fire was rifle and machine gun, this of course Colonel Collison was grateful for but did fuel his already low estimation of the standard of German infantry.

This type of pioneering work was continued until they returned to Humbercamps on 12th September. One addition to the communication trenches which the 11th were making, is a system called feathers or slits. These additions were narrow, deep channels about 20 yards long cut at right angles from the trench wall, they were designed to accommodate men in the trench waiting to relieve their counterparts in the front line.

It was particularly wet now and written orders were drawn up to accommodate the relief operations. Many trenches were not floor boarded so there was a continual slog through mud when moving along the trenches, to assist with this, rubber galoshes had been made available in limited numbers and the instructions for men being relieved were to hand their boots tied in pairs to an NCO who would in turn hand them to a counterpart in the relieving units who would then distribute them to his men.

The system of holding the front now was two companies holding the line, with two in reserve. After six days these companies swapped roles. The companies in reserve were responsible for taking food and beverages to the men in the fire trenches and listening posts and recovering the empty Billy tins: under no circumstances could a soldier in a fire trench leave his post. At the end of the second period of six days all four companies were relieved and went to the rear in Divisional reserve for 12 days, this was referred to as rest period or more commonly, out of trench period. In the evenings after dark a transport vehicle clattered along the roads to bring provisions and the daily post. Every now and then German artillery would target the road along which the vehicle was travelling resulting in the loss of that night's treats, our artillery would retaliate of course making the German gunners think twice about their action.

Zachariah had been allocated to a machine gun crew and on 3rd September 1915 a nasty incident occurred when one of the gunners, Private Livesey, accidentally blew off his left thumb with his rifle. Just after this incident the 11th came out of the trenches and returned to Humbercamps where they rested in the daytime and formed working parties digging trenches at night. During the night of September 15th 1915, the 11th took over trenches near Hannescamps from 13th Royal Fusiliers, the changeover completed without incident by 01.15 a.m. The following day another accident occurred when a man was killed by a rifle being fired near to him and on 19th an officer was injured when he slipped returning to the trenches from a reconnoitre of the German line and fell on a sentry's bayonet.

At about 5.30 p.m. on 24th September 1915, Zachariah was on duty at his machine gun, located in a dugout, when several shells were fired from a German Howitzer, one of these rounds scored a direct hit on the dugout killing Zachariah instantly and severely injuring three other men. Zachariah was buried in Bienvillers Military Cemetery on 25th September, he was awarded the 1914-15 Star, Victory and British War Medals.

Chapter 13

Charles Houghton

In August 1914 Charles Houghton was living in Polesworth and working at Pooley Hall colliery as a Hewer. Following the call to Arms Charles, aged at least 40 years, attended his local recruitment station and volunteered for service with the South Staffordshire Regiment. Even though the recruitment stations were turning away volunteers for any small reason, since the system was overloaded by the incredible response to the call to arms, Charles was eagerly accepted and posted to the South Staffordshire regiment as Private 10158, for the very good reason that he was a time served soldier with good experience which could be put to good use.

Charles was baptised on 12th March 1874, at St Michael's Church, Brereton, Staffordshire. His date of birth is unknown and records vary between 1872 and 1874. His parents were George Houghton, a miner, and Eliza Houghton, who by 1881 had housed their family at 51, Redbrook Lane, Rugeley, Staffordshire. Charles had six siblings whose ages ranged from 16 to six, and his age is recorded as seven. In 1891, Charles at 19, is still living with his parents and four siblings at the same address and he is employed as an Iron Moulder, making the moulds for casting iron.

On 21st August 1894, Charles joined the army at Lichfield and was accepted into the South Staffordshire Regiment as Private

4238. Charles already had military training as he had served as a volunteer with 2nd (Volunteer) Battalion Staffordshire Yeomanry, he even had a tattoo on his left forearm of the crown and knot which constituted the cap badge of this territorial unit.

Staffordshire knot Tattoo; Picture courtesy of Mr Lee Paul Philip Curtis who chose this design to honour his brother Philip Dale Rhimes Hewett KIA in Afghanistan.

In addition to the tattoo, the medical examination of Charles showed that he was 20 years and seven months old, 5'6" tall, 133 lbs with a chest expansion of 2" to a maximum of 36", he had grey eyes, a fresh complexion and light brown hair.

From his joining date until 11th December 1895, Charles served with 1st and 2nd Battalions in England and then, on 12th December 1895, he was posted to India. Whilst helping to guard the Empire, Charles learnt to play the drum and was accordingly posted as a Bandsman on 29th August 1899. He resigned this position for a short time in December 1900 but re-joined the band in September 1901. On 21st August 1903, Bandsman 4238 Houghton was placed on the Army reserve list and presumably left the South Staffordshire regiment to find his way in civilian life. On 20th August 1906, his record shows that he was discharged from the army having served his allotted time which amounted to 12 years.

The census of 1911 records Charles as now out of the army and living as a lodger at New Street, Polesworth with the family of John Wright. Both men were employed at the Pooley

Hall Colliery as Hewers. A 1917 report states that Charles had been living in Polesworth for 12 years prior to joining up in 1914 and was a well-liked and respected man.

Charles's military record relating to his World War Iservice has not survived, but from accounts in newspapers following his death, we know that he enlisted in August 1914 into the South Staffordshire Regiment but was not posted to France until March 1916 when he joined the 8th Battalion. Because he was so readily accepted by the recruitment system in 1914, because of his age and experience, following (or perhaps even during basic training) it is likely that he was elevated to Lance Corporal and then Corporal to assist with the training of the many volunteers who had no experience of military life. The 3rd Battalion of the South Staffordshire Regiment was a training unit and remained in England throughout the war. Originally formed in Lichfield in August 1914, which coincides with Charles's re-enlistment, it moved first to Plymouth and then, in May 1915, to Sunderland. This was probably his first posting as a trainer until, by virtue of the extreme shortage of fighting men, he managed to get himself assigned to a fighting unit. Charles was promoted to Sergeant in January 1916 and transferred to 8th Battalion who had been fighting in France since 1915, having landed at Boulogne on 14th July, Bastille Day.

Almost as soon as he arrived in the trenches, Charles was bitten by a louse and contracted Trench Fever. This disease was relatively common and somewhere between one fifth and one third of British troops became infected. The illness has a two-week incubating period followed by five days of high fever, severe headache, pain on moving the eyeballs, soreness of the muscles of the legs and back. It rarely resulted in death but recovery can be a month or more. Charles's case became severe and he was invalided back to a hospital in Plymouth in August 1915. Looking at the time frame between him going to France and being shipped back to England, if he actually arrived at the fighting front it was for a very small period. From the hospital in Plymouth he was transferred to Ripon Army Camp Hospital where, on 25th February 1917, he died of Pleurisy.

On Saturday 3rd March 1917, Sgt 10158 Charles Houghton of South Staffordshire Regiment was buried with full military honours at the church where he was christened, St Michaels, Brereton, Staffordshire. He had remained a single man and was awarded the British War and Victory Medals.

Chapter 14

Arthur Jackson

By 1891 Henry and Fanny Jackson's family was complete. They were living at 24 Seckington Lane, Newton Regis, Warwickshire, with their four children and one grandchild. Arthur was the youngest child aged five and Henry was employed as a Groom/Coachman. By 1901, Arthur at 16, was living with his Farmer employer at More Burgess Farm, Tamworth, and was employed as a Waggoner and farm worker. In 1909, Arthur married Mary Riley in Newton Regis on Boxing Day, nine months later the couple were blessed by the birth of a daughter, Rhoda. The family address is simply recorded as Newton Regis which is a small community near to Polesworth where Arthur was employed at the Pooley Hall Colliery as an underground Hewer.

Between 1911, when Arthur was employed at Pooley Hall Colliery, and 1914, he changed career again and joined the South Staffordshire Regiment; he was posted to 2nd Battalion as Private 7167. While Arthur's military file no longer exists, we can safely make this assumption as the 2nd Battalion was a professional unit, in existence since 1st July 1881.Immediately following the outbreak of World War I the Battalion was mobilised to France. There was no time to take on board fresh recruits who had volunteered because of the war. Arthur was a Lance Corporal and, therefore, a fully trained soldier with sufficient experience and personality to take the first steps to leadership. The 2nd Battalion had served around the Empire but in 1911 it had returned to England from service in Pretoria South Africa and was based at Aldershot. Perhaps the news that this regiment had returned to England from exotic locations had prompted Arthur to give up the hard and dangerous work underground for something more glamorous!

On 4th August 1914, the commanding officer of 2nd Battalion, Lieutenant Colonel C.S. Davidson, received orders to mobilise for transportation to France with the British Expeditionary Force (BEF). On 6th August, the Battalion was ready and eagerly awaiting orders. During the very early hours of 12thAugust, two trains took the Battalion from Aldershot to Southampton where they boarded the SS Irrawaddy and set sail for France at 1.30 p.m. They disembarked at Le Havre at 7.30 a.m. the following day and marched to Number One camp arriving there at 10.30 a.m., again they waited for further orders. On 15th August those orders having arrived, the Battalion moved by train and march to Iron, where they went into billets and awaited orders. On 21st August, the men started a three day march to Harmingies arriving there at 11 a.m. on 23rd. Here they experienced enemy fire for the first time, the village was brought to a state of defence and trenches were prepared and manned. That night an artillery battle was fought and at 2 a.m. orders were received to retire; German forces were advancing and the Battalion's role was to retire and cover the retreat of the rest of the Brigade. After a very long day on 24thAugust, which was extremely hot, the Battalion arrived at Bauay where they were ordered to entrench and form a defensive line. The men dug throughout the night. With the 1st King's Liverpool Regiment, the Battalion held their positions all day while the rest of the Brigade retired to Marroilles, there was little fighting and they had received no casualties to date. The two Battalions then also retired to Marroilles, arriving early evening on 25th August 1914 and were placed in billets in the town for a well-earned rest. Unfortunately, at 8 p.m., an order was received to 'stand to arms' as the Germans had arrived at the edge of the town. Nobody had any sleep that night and the following day the Battalion again retired on a march lasting until 6.30 p.m. 31st August 1914 when they arrived at Ambleny. By now the men were exhausted having marched by day and either finding billets or bivouacking at night, but there was to be no rest as the Battalion went into defensive positions covering the south of the village.

On 1st September 1914, the retreat continued but at 2.15.p.m. that day, a report was received that 4th Guards Brigade, who were engaged in a rear-guard action, had been heavily attacked by the Germans and had suffered losses. The 6th Infantry Brigade, which included Arthur's Battalion, turned around to support the rear guard assisted by the 34thBrigade, Royal Field Artillery. The 2nd Battalion took up position on the right of the Guards in a wood and at 4 p.m. were subjected to a heavy artillery bombardment from the Germans lasting over one hour. The Battalion records its first casualties; one man killed and 24 wounded. At 6 p.m. the men went on the move again, retreating to Thury-en-Valois arriving at 10 p.m. where they bivouacked. This first rest for days was not to last long, for at 3.30 a.m., 2nd September 1914, they continued their march which became a daily routine from village to village camping or finding billets at night, heading in a Southerly direction around the east side of Paris. At 8.45 a.m. on 10th September 1914, the Battalion encountered a German column and immediately attacked. The fighting lasted for 2½ hours and resulted in 450 Germans surrendering and being taken prisoner. The Battalion's casualties were one man killed and two officers and five other ranks wounded. Following the fighting, the men advanced two miles to the village of Chevillion where they bivouacked for the night.

The daily march continued until they reached Moussy, south of Dijon, on 14th September 1914. Here it was found that the Germans had taken up strong positions and the 2nd Battalion was kept at Moussy as Divisional reserve. Even in a reserve position the danger was present and they were targeted by artillery fire suffering several casualties. On 16th September, the

Battalion was sent to support the 4th Guards Brigade at Soupir, on the way two men were killed and seven injured. On arrival, they were sent back to Moussy, but then on 19th September were sent back as a reserve force for the Guards at Soupir. The diary notes that although the weather had been good it now started to rain heavily, but on a good note supplies had been arriving on a regular basis and the fitness of the men was very high.

On 20th September 1914, the Battalion was split into two, C & D Companies took over front line trenches from 1st Kings Royal Rifles and A & D Companies were sent to Cavonne to support the Wiltshire Regiment. More casualties were experienced; one man killed and seven wounded. The same day, A & D Companies returned to Cavonne and the two sets of companies relieved each other in the front line held there. On 22nd September 1914, the Battalion left the line and moved into billets for a rest at Bourg, but not for long, as on 25th September they returned to Soupir and took up positions in the front line. The following day the Battalion's Royal Army Medical Corps (RAMC) Doctor, Lieutenant William Ormsby Wyndham Ball, was killed in action, his body was not identified, but he was later commemorated on the memorial at La Ferte-Sous-Jouarre Memorial.

Between 21st August and 5th September, Arthur and his comrades had marched 236 miles during the retirement from Belgium; an average of 15.7 miles per day with only six days' rest. Since the 5th September the action was to create a defensive wall preventing the Germans from attaining their goal, Paris. It is an accolade to the support services of the British Army that throughout this seemingly chaotic period the men were kept adequately supplied with ammunition, food and other essential supplies.

The first half of October 1914 was spent in front line trenches but on 15th October, they were relieved by the French 148th

Regiment and marched to Fisnes, where, on the following day, they boarded trains for destinations unknown. The train journey lasted two days, passing through, Amiens, Boulogne and Calais, finally arriving at Strazelle at midnight on 17th October 1914. From here the men were marched to billets at Hazebrouck. The Battalion was engaged in numerous engagements with the enemy over the next two months and experienced many casualties. On one occasion the Germans broke through the French lines on the Battalion's left flank and fierce fighting managed to secure what had been a critical situation. On 3rd December 1914, the Brigade whilst in billets at Caestre, were visited and inspected by His Majesty the King. The Battalion was rested at this location until 22nd December 1914 when they were driven in motor buses of the London General Omnibus Co. to Bethune from where they marched to Beuvry where they again took their turn in the front-line trenches.

It was in these front lines that Arthur celebrated Christmas 1914, the diary merely mentions that the period was quiet and they were hardly bothered by shelling, but there was the persistent menace from snipers. The run up to Christmas 1914 had involved large scale organisation back in Britain to ensure that the lads at the front were not forgotten. People were encouraged to donate gifts, food, and clothing whilst others frantically knitted scarves and other warm items to ensure that the army was as comfortable as possible and felt in touch with home. There is no mention of any fraternisation with the enemy as experienced in other parts of the front, with football matches, cigarette exchange or competitive carol singing, but it is difficult to imagine that the men did not celebrate in some small way to enjoy the quiet spell from the many dangers of trench warfare and to raise their own spirits. During the afternoon of Boxing Day 1914, the Battalion was relieved by 2nd Royal Sussex Regiment and went into billets at Essars.

January and February 1915, were spent in and out of the front-line trenches, the static nature of trench warfare had started and would be largely how the First World War would be remembered. A rotation system was in place where a Battalion was split into two, both halves being assigned to another Battalion to make six companies operating a relief system. Two companies of the Glasgow Highlanders were assigned to 2nd Battalion South Staffordshire Regiment and each pair of companies spent 48 hours in the front line before being relieved.

On 10th March 1915, Arthur was involved in a brigade attack against the German positions North East of Givenchy. An artillery bombardment commenced at 7.30 a.m. and at 8.10 a.m., the Infantry moved forward. The advance was on a three-column front. On the right were three Companies of the 2nd South Staffordshire Regiment, led by B Company and supported by C and A Companies under the overall command of the Battalion Commander Lieutenant Colonel Routledge. The centre column were three companies of the 1st King's (Liverpool) Regiment and, on the left, were three companies of the 1st King's Royal Rifle Corps.

The story is now best told by Lieutenant Colonel Routledge himself:

At 8.10 a.m. B Coy. Advanced against the enemy's trenches in front of Duck's Bill just East of Givenchy. The advance commenced from three previously prepared points in our line where traverses had been built by the E. ANGLIAN FIELD Coy. R.E. (Territorials) and a portion of the parapet knocked down to enable the men to leave the trench. A certain amount of our wire which consisted of knife rest frames just in front of the parapet, had been removed during the previous night to enable the men to pass through it. As soon as the men left the shelter of our parapet they were subjected to a very severe cross fire from machine guns (2) in the German trench which at this point was 80 yards distant from our own. A certain number of men reached the German trench but were unable to remain there. 2/Lieut. Hewat and 15 men attacked with the object of capturing a machine gun which was doing great execution but none of them returned. 2/Lieut. Wood with about 12 men got into the German trench on the right but they were bombed out by the enemy. 2/Lieut. Wood then headed another party and a platoon of C Coy. Under 2/Lieut. Richards was also sent forward; but no permanent lodgement could be effected in the enemy's trenches. Eventually the attack ceased and the right column was ordered to reform.

About 1 p.m. orders were received from Bde. That a fresh bombardment would take place at 2.15 p.m. followed by a fresh assault at 2.45.p.m. & the right column was to have one coy. 1/Royal Berkshire Regt. As a support. Another \ coy. 1/R. Berks was to deliver an assault between the right column and the centre column if the German wire was cut by our artillery fire. C Coy. was told off to lead the assault supported by A Coy. B Coy. which had suffered very heavily in the morning being withdrawn. C Coy. remained in occupation of our front line, A Coy having withdrawn to the MAIRIE REDOUBT and a communication trench leading thence to the front line of trenches. The men had what food they had been able to carry with them.

The OC C Coy. conferred with the OC B Coy. and made arrangements for the fresh assault. Since the Germans had their machine guns trained on the positions from which previous assaulting parties had eft our trenches it was decided that the men should get over the parapet by means of sandbag steps erected in different parts of the line. The attack was to be made by 2 Platoons of C Coy in front line, supported immediately by the other 2 Platoons, A coy. to follow in the same order owing to the fact that sufficient of our wire had not been removed, each platoon could only start on a frontage of 1 section.

The bombardment commenced at 2.15 p.m. and at 2.45 p.m. the leading sections advanced only to be mown down by machine gun fire as soon as they had surmounted our parapet. Meanwhile a proportion of the Berkshire Coy., which was to assault on our left, rushed into the communication trench by which the supports were to come up and had blocked A Coy who were thus unable to support C Coy. closely. The German wire not having been cut and their trenches having apparently suffered very slightly from the preliminary bombardment, it was decided after consultation between OC right column and the OC R. BERKSHIRE Regt. who was directing the movements of his intermediate column not to press the assault further. A report was sent to the VI Brigade and about 3.45 p.m. orders were received to reform the garrison (D Coy.) along the old trench line and the assaulting column under cover in rear, the R. Berkshires being ordered to clear our communication. This was done and the column formed up in the following order A Coy. leading, C Coy., B Coy. About 4 p.m. orders were received to repair the trenches with the assistance of the R.E. and to collect all the wounded and their equipment. This work was continued till a late hour, the stretcher bearers very hard to remove all the casualties. In the action the Battalion suffered the following losses.

<u>Killed</u>

Lieut. G.E.A. PARKER. Lieut. L.F.YEO (Died of wounds)

2/Lieut. H.C. STONER

2/Lieut. A.D.SPRUNT (Died of wounds 17-3-15)

And 24 Other Ranks.

<u>*Wounded*</u>

Lieut. J.S. TOWNSEND 2/Lieut. R.J.P. RICHARDSON

And 74 Other Ranks.

<u>*MISSING*</u>

2/Lieut G.M.F. HEWAT and 33 Other Ranks.

Arthur did not return with the survivors and his body was never identified, he was counted in the missing statistic and his family informed that he was missing presumed dead.

At midnight on 10th March 1915, three Companies of the 2nd South Staffs were relieved, D Company remained in situ, the new plan being to renew the attack at 7.30 a.m., 11th March. The renewed attack was never pressed and the Battalion went into reserve for refit and supply, within days they received a replacement draft of 15 officers and 226 Other Ranks, they then went back into the line and for them the war continued.

Arthur's financial account was not settled for over a year, but he left £4.13s.4d. which was supplemented by a £5 War Gratuity which was eventually given to his wife. After his death, Mary received a portion of his wage to prevent destitution and eventually a war pension. Arthur's memory is honoured on the Le Touret Memorial which commemorates over 13,400 British soldiers who were killed in this sector of the Western Front from the beginning of October 1914, to the eve of the Battle of Loos in late September 1915 and who have no known grave. It is situated in the Le Touret Military Cemetery, on the Bethune to Armetiers road Pas de Calais. Arthur was awarded the 1914 Star, Victory and British War medals.

Chapter 15

William Jacobs

What records that exist concerning William give no indication that he was connected to the mining industry. He was born in 1893 in Walton-on-Trent, Staffordshire and his father, James, was an Agricultural Labourer. William's mother, Elizabeth, had given birth to six children by 1901 and the family lived at Hames Lane, Newton Regis, Warwickshire, which is just a few miles away from Pooley Hall Colliery; a tenuous connection. William was the fourth successive boy, the elder two, aged 19 and 13, were a Blacksmith's Apprentice and a Carter's Lad on a farm respectively and his two younger siblings were both girls. Ten years later, William is now resident with, and employed by, Edward White, a Joiner and Wheelwright, at Netherseal, Ashby de la Zouch, Leicestershire. Edward White's family consisted of his wife Elizabeth and their two daughters, both of whom were at school, and William was in Edward's employ as a General Labourer and Wheelwright. At some stage during the next few years William, changed career direction and became employed at Pooley Hall Colliery, but in an unknown capacity.

At some stage during 1915, probably early in the year (an assumption made from his subsequent War Gratuity), William joined the army and was posted as Private 34086 to 9th (Service) Battalion, Worcestershire Regiment. This Unit had been formed at Worcester in August 1914 and in June 1915 sailed from

Avonmouth to Gallipoli. In January 1916, it was evacuated from Gallipoli and transferred to the North Persia Force in Mesopotamia, where William joined his Battalion with a draft of new recruits and returnees from hospital or leave.

On 6th September 1918, the 9th Battalion having been billeted in the town of Baku, Azerbaijan, went into front line trenches at Balajari, three miles north of Baku. The situation had been quiet recently and the men had been involved with controlling refugees from Russia and Armenia, containing them in a refugee camp and removing weapons and ammunition from them. Patrols were sent out at night and dawn to report on Turkish movements, the night patrol for 9th September reported seeing an enemy Piquet of about 30 rifles, 1000 yards north of the front line (In this context Piquet used to describe a unit of troops). The same patrol had also found a quantity of equipment lost by the 7th North Staffords on a previous encounter with the Turkish forces. The following night a strong patrol was sent out and successfully recovered all of this lost equipment. A night patrol on 11[th]September, reported an encounter with the enemy who had fired on them. They had withdrawn without casualties as the enemy Piquet was judged to be in force. The following night a strong patrol was sent to attack this unit but because of formidable defences had to settle for throwing all their grenades from a 30 yard distance and retiring under fire.

Information was received that the enemy were planning to attack in force on the morning of the 14th September 1918 and in readiness the front line was reinforced and additional ammunition and bombs were allocated to the defenders. At 4.15 a.m., the Russian and Armenian forces situated to the right of the 9th were subjected to heavy rifle fire and bombing attacks, followed very soon by an attack on one of the 9th's positions by 50 enemy riflemen, this attack was beaten back with the only loss being to the enemy. At 6 a.m. a large enemy force was seen concentrating but was dispersed into smaller groups by effective Vickers and Lewis machine gun fire. The main Turkish force attacked the Allied line to the left of the 9th Battalion's positions which was held by Armenian troops. At 8.30 a.m., a report was received that the Turks had broken through and were advancing on Baku; a grave situation. The 9th Battalion was in danger of being attacked from the rear and to counter that threat, posted a Company to its rear on high ground. During the morning, this Company became heavily engaged with the Turkish forces and suffered heavy losses. At 12.50 p.m. orders were received to retire from the front line to high ground 600 yards to the rear this took a few hours to achieve as they were forced to fight their way through an enemy determined to cut them off and destroy them. One British other rank (BOR) was killed and several officers and men wounded. Further orders were received to retire another 800 yards and link with the 9th Royal Warwick's and hold the ridge at that location. At 4 p.m. orders were now received that all British Forces were to be evacuated from Baku by sea, the Battalions formed up and marched through the town to the harbour where they boarded ships and sailed out to sea. During the evacuation through the town and at sea, the men were warned to expect resistance to them leaving by the people of Baku and then Russian Gun Boats stationed in the harbour. Fortunately, there was no problems encountered and the whole 39th Brigade was successfully evacuated without the loss of men and equipment.

The casualties suffered by 9th Battalion were; two BORs killed, two wounded, nine wounded and missing, 15 missing. William was amongst one of the two missing categories and was ultimately declared, 'presumed dead'. He left a total of £37.10s.0d, which included a war gratuity of £13.10s.0d. to his father, James. He was awarded the British War and Victory Medals and his name was engraved on the Tehran War Memorial. This Memorial is part of the Commonwealth War Cemeteries situated in modern day Iran. It has graves for 563

Commonwealth sailors, soldiers and airmen and one nursing sister killed in both World Wars, also the memorial commemorates 3,590 other servicemen, killed but having no known grave. The Cemetery forms part of the grounds occupied by the British Embassy in Tehran.

Chapter 16

Frank Lees

Frank's military career did not start very well at all; he was conscripted at the beginning of 1916 and was inducted into the 11thBattalion, North Staffordshire Regiment as Private 18689. Whilst his military file no longer exists there is some evidence which dates his movements. The 11th (Reserve) Battalion was formed in Guernsey in October 1914 and moved to Alderney the following year. It remained in the UK throughout the war and served as a training Battalion for the North Staffordshire Regiment. By 1916, the Battalion was stationed at Rugeley, Cannock Chase, and was designated as 3rd Training Reserve Battalion. Frank managed to get a pass home which expired on 22nd January 1916 at midnight, but he was seen by Police Constable Stone after that date and Frank promised to return to camp on the next train. He did not, so PC Stone arrested him and arranged a military escort. This incident made news in the Tamworth Herald on 29th January 1916. Frank returned to his Battalion, finished his training and was then posted to the 8th Battalion North Staffordshire Regiment, who were now serving in France.

Frank was born in 1884 in Two Gates Tamworth, on 20th March and baptised the same year at Holy Trinity Church, Wilnecote. His parents were James and Frances Lees, Frank was their fifth child and four years later Frances gave birth to a son, James, but tragically died between giving birth and the

1891 Census. At the time of this Census, James, a coal miner, had housed his seven children at Halls Row, Tamworth and his two eldest children, daughters, were employed as a Tailoress (as described on the census) and a Silk Weaver; the other children were in school or below school age. By 1901, Frank had moved to live with his Uncle, John Lees at Quarry Road, Polesworth. John Lees, also a Coal Miner, was employed at the Pooley Hall Colliery as a Hewer. Frank, now 17 years old, also worked at Pooley Hall as an Underground Horse Driver. In 1906, Frank married Jessie Lycett in Tamworth and by 1911 the couple were childless but living at 3, Anchor Road, Glascote, Tamworth and he was now employed as a Hewer.

I think we can draw a firm conclusion from the above which puts his bad start in the Army into clear perspective. Frank was a hardworking man, brought up with a strong family loyalty ethic and his absenteeism is undoubtedly in response to a family crisis. It is highly unlikely that at such an early stage in his military training he would have been given a pass home without it being for compassionate reasons and once home found it extremely difficult to comply with his instruction to return. Men in the various theatres of war were shot at dawn for much less and there is no doubt his continued absenteeism would have been taken very seriously.

Dependant on what punishment was given to Frank on his return to Camp on Cannock Chase, depends on when he had completed his training and sent to his unit in the field. Every man was needed for the 'Big Push' as the offensive of the Battle of the Somme was called and it is likely he was with the 8th by 1stJuly, 1916. In fact a draft of 82 men arrived with the Battalion on 25th May, perhaps he was with this group. At this time, the Battalion was based at St Riquier, east of Abbeyville in the Somme District. It was engaged in training for trench attack; advancing from assembly trenches in artillery formation, capturing an enemy position and then consolidating it in readiness to repel counter attack. It was essential in these broad front attacks to keep the individual units in a cohesive line, otherwise a flank is presented to the enemy giving opportunity to break through and cut them off from any support. Caught in encirclement, it is then only a matter of time before the trapped forces are destroyed. This often created a situation where units who had pushed further forward than their neighbours, would have to retire to a more defendable position. On 30th June 1916, the Battalion marched to the Corps reserve line to await their turn take part in the forthcoming battle. The artillery bombardment of the German lines had been ongoing for seven days and over 1.7 million artillery shells of all sizes had been fired to cut the German wire, destroy the enemies front line positions and kill the enemy therein.

For the 1st July, the diary makes an interesting observation. Each soldier carried arms and equipment, including rations, which weighed a total of 69 lbs. The field manual stated that this weight should not exceed 59 lbs. Men were being required to walk forward in a controlled line into the face of machine-gun, sniper, artillery and mortar fire, carrying a very heavy load. This does give an indication of the reliance being placed on the effectiveness of the artillery bombardment which was only lifted at 7.30 a.m. on the 1st July 1916, which was the moment the whistles sounded and the infantry commenced their attack. The 8th waited in their positions but could see nothing; perhaps that was for the best, as on this first day across the whole front of the battle, 60,000 casualties occurred of which almost 20,000 were fatalities.

During this 1st day of the battle, the 8th Battalion moved forward in stages until they were next to go. At 8 p.m. they received orders to go into attack and bomb La Boiselle. At 10.30 p.m. when they arrived at the necessary communication trenches to get into position, they found them blocked with wounded and displaced men and consequently did not get to the designated start point until 4.30 a.m. the next day. The attack was cancelled. That night, 2nd July 1916, the same orders came back with an assurance that the communication trenches were cleared of casualties. This was not the case and many stretcher cases hampered the Battalion's advance. On this occasion, they were successful and at 4.05 a.m., 3rd July, launched a bombing attack on the village of La Boiselle. 24 bombing parties led the attack and made good progress through the enemy positions, at a point three quarters of the way through the village, despite the best efforts of carrying parties, the bomb supply started to run out. Snipers had been very active during the attack and had successfully targeted officers directing operations, there were also about 100 prisoners taken which complicated matters as they had to be guarded and escorted back to British lines. A counter attack by the enemy was launched and the 8th pushed back to a point about one quarter of the way through the village. They were joined by two Companies of the Warwickshire Regiment and together the German counter attack was broken and forced back. More bombs and men arrived but attack and counter attack resulted in the line being held about half way through the village by 12 noon that day and this was held until the Battalion was relieved at 6 a.m. the following morning, 4th July 1916. The Battalion retired to the old British front line and rested there for the day, heavy rain in the afternoon and evening made the trenches waterlogged. At 8 p.m., 5th July 1916, the Battalion arrived in Billets at Albert, drenched, filthy and tired. The survivors commenced the task of cleaning themselves and equipment in readiness for the next action. Casualties from this action were; four officers and 28 other ranks killed, eight officers and 210 other ranks wounded, 34 other ranks missing, 790 men started the attack, 506 men returned of which Frank was one.

On 8th July 1916, the Battalion with its depleted strength, was sent back into the line to hold positions near to Bapaume where they were to meet guides. The guides were uncertain exactly where to take them as the line had moved forward in the preceding days 600 yards, eventually they were in position at 5.30 a.m. the following day. The line was held, the men enduring constant artillery attack and attack by enemy bombing parties, until 5 p.m., 10th July 1916, suffering a further 60 casualties.

From 11th July to 19th July 1916, the Battalion rested and practised bombing techniques with the Lewis Gun teams. On 19th, a draft of two 2nd Lieutenants and 114 other ranks was received, orders were received to return to the offensive and the Battalion prepared to take part in the second phase of the Somme Offensive, the Battle for Delville Wood. The centre point of this battle was the high lying areas of High Wood and Poziéres. The 8th Battalion North Staffordshire Regiment, were concentrating on taking the ground between High Wood and the village of Bazentin-Le-Petit. On the night of 19th July 1916, the men bivouacked in Becourt Wood and the following evening marched up to relieve the front line. There was continual heavy shelling throughout this relief and guides had to take a route across country rather than in communication trenches, because of this shelling, heavy casualties were taken before even getting to the fighting positions and this time Frank's luck had run out; he was killed and his body never recovered. The Battalion was involved in combat until relieved on 24th July 1916 and the casualties are recorded as; ten officers wounded, of which one later died of his wounds, other ranks; 18 killed, 89 wounded, 24 missing, of which Frank was one and later reported killed in action.

Frank left £2.15s.1d. which was added to with a war gratuity of £3 (indicating less than one year of service which fits with the above facts), left to his widow Jessie. Frank was awarded the British War and Victory Medals for his sacrifice and his name subsequently engraved on both the Thiepval and Pooley Hall Colliery Memorials.

Chapter 17

Charles Nash

Charles Nash is commemorated on the Pooley Hall Colliery Memorial at Polesworth. Unfortunately, the work of several researchers has been unable to identify who this individual was. In the available records, there are 26 casualties named Charles Nash, but none have an apparent connection to the Polesworth area. Of these 26 there are only four simply named Charles Nash the other 22 have a middle name. The Polesworth memorial is accurate on all other names, where there is a middle name the initial is also engraved, I strongly suspect that Charles is one of the following men (details as per Commonwealth War Graves Commission records):

1. Private 24304 Charles Nash, died on 27th February 1917 aged 34 of 7th Battalion Royal Dublin Fusiliers. Buried in Salonika (Lembet Road), Military Cemetery. The son of George and Catherine Nash of London.
2. Rifleman R14558 Charles Nash, died Monday 23rd April 1917 of 16th Battalion Kings Royal Rifle Corps. Commemorated on the Arras Memorial.
3. Leading Stoker 295025 Charles Nash, died 7th January 1915 aged 34 of H.M. S/M "C31" Royal Navy. Son of Eli and Louisa Nash, husband of Annie Nash of Woodmancote Emsworth Hants.
4. Sapper 504580 Charles Nash died 19th October 1918 of 63rd Field Company Royal Engineers. Son of James

Robert and Elizabeth Nash 21, Longground, Frome (Born Warminster).

My assumption may be totally wrong of course, records are as good as the input information, for instance in respect of number 3: the submarine HMS C31 was sunk by a mine on 4th January 1915 with the loss of all hands and not on 7th January as stated above.

For the time being Charles Nash must remain a name on a Memorial and is a stark reminder to us that these men made the ultimate sacrifice in the fight for freedom and must never be forgotten. I gladly give him a page in this book to honour his memory and can only hope that one day someone will stumble across a document we have missed to date and set the record straight as to who this hero was!

Chapter 18

Arthur Herbert Owen
&
George Frederick Turner

These two men's stories are linked in a number of ways. They were both miners at Pooley Hall Colliery, they were both killed in the same action, whilst serving with the same Battalion and neither have a known grave but are commemorated on the Thiepval Memorial near Albert in France.

Arthur Herbert Owen was born in Grendon, Warwickshire in 1897. No accurate record of his birth date exists the record merely states he was born in the first quarter. In 1901, his family consisted of; his father, Joseph, a farmer and pork butcher - his mother Mary - two elder brothers - a younger sister and his grandfather Richard Owen - a 74 year old widower and retired farmer. The family home was 86, Brookside, Witherley, near Atherstone. Arthur was four at the time of this census and the person recording the details for this road had confused names and he is recorded as Arthur Edward Owen. Mother Mary was born in Leicestershire and all her children are shown as born in Ratcliffe Culey, Leicestershire, a nearby village and presumably where Mary had female relatives where she could retreat to for her confinement.

In 1911 the family had moved to 'Rosemount', Orton on the Hill, Atherstone. One additional daughter is added to the family total but Grandfather Richard is no longer shown. Arthur, now 14, is working as a Grocers Assistant and father is now working as a Coal Miner, specifically a Hewer. This location is easily in walking distance from Pooley Hall Colliery and no doubt at some stage prior to World War I, where Arthur sought employment prior to joining the army.

George Frederick Turner was born in 1898 in Fisherwick, Staffordshire, to Frederick and Lucy Turner. In 1901 George, at the age of three, was resident with his grandparents, John and Mary Collins, in a cottage in what we now know as The Packington Hall Estate. John was a cattle farmer. In 1911, George was now back with his own family at 50, Albion Street, Tamworth. At the age of 12 he was the first of eight children and this may well have been why in 1901, at the age of only three, he was with his grandparents whilst a sibling was born. The 1911 record, shows that eight children had been born alive and all had survived to that date, there was, however, no requirement to register the birth of still born children. Frederick was employed as a miner but no profession is shown for the only two other persons eligible for work, Lucy and George who may have still been in school.

There being no other records, we must assume that George followed his father into the coal mining industry and was employed at Pooley Hall Colliery. The only other clues to piece together George's story are somewhat devoid of detail. His military file does not exist and his medal card merely shows his number, Battalion and entitlement to the British War and Victory medals, it does not give a date of entitlement which would have told us when George entered the theatre of war which qualified him for the awards. Two other records exist; the register of soldiers' effects and the medal award register. All records show that he was Private 11782 of 1st Battalion, Royal Warwickshire Regiment but the register of medal awards also shows he was first a member of 2nd Battalion, Royal Warwickshire Regiment. I believe this to be a wrong entry and should show that he was first assigned to the 3rd Battalion which was the training Battalion for the Royal Warwickshire Regiment. The 2nd Battalion was sent to France in October 1914 and would not have been used to train recruits in the field. The only other records relating to George are concerning his death which is linked to Arthur Owen and we can resume the story with him.

Arthur's military file has not survived but his medal card shows he was a member of the 1st Battalion Royal Warwickshire Regiment and that he entered the French theatre of war on 13th July 1915. In 1915, Arthur was 18 years of age. Conscription was not introduced until 1916, so we can state that he was a volunteer at his earliest legal time if not before. On enlistment at Atherstone, Warwickshire, he was assigned the number 10555 and as the 1st Battalion mobilised to France on 22nd August 1914, we can assume he was sent to the 3rd Battalion for his basic training - the 3rd being the reserve Battalion formed in August 1914 and initially housed at Portsmouth, then the Isle of Wight and finally Dover in 1917. Whilst training content and length varied Arthur would have completed a minimum of three months basic training before being assigned to a Battalion where he would receive further, more advanced and specialist instruction. As the 1st Battalion was already in France, it is likely he was sent to join the 1st after his three months basic which gives us an approximate joining date of early April 1915 which would coincide with his 18th birthday which is recorded in the first quarter.

When Arthur arrived in the field on 28th July 1915, the 1st Battalion were in trenches at Sucrerie near to Mailly-Maillet having entered these positions two days previously. There was a steady flow of casualties occurring from sniper fire and

'Little Willies', the smallest German artillery shell. The name was an official description distributed to all units for use of reporting enemy artillery in an effort to coordinate description and thereby gain an accurate intelligence picture of the quantity and quality of enemy artillery pieces. The descriptions were in ascending size, Little Willie, White Hopes, Portmanteaus, Coal Boxes, Black Marias, and Jack Johnsons. On each occasion the French Artillery responded with 75mm artillery pieces which made the enemy cease fire. Arthur arrived with a draft of four officers and 106 other ranks, this no doubt was a welcome addition to the strength, which had been counted just before entering the line as, 20 officers and 863 other ranks, quite low for Battalion strength. A few days later a further draft of 115 men arrived with three 2nd Lieutenants. There is a very interesting tally table at this point in the diary and it serves as a good example of the level of casualties which had occurred in a front line infantry Battalion since the start of the war;

Officers served with the battalion;	*Killed 20*
	Wounded 23
	Missing & prisoners of war 9
Approximate numbers of NCOs & men;	*Killed 324*
	Wounded 1060
	Missing & prisoners of war 381

The 1st remained in these trenches until 8th August 1915, when they were relieved at 9.30 p.m. by the Royal Dublin fusiliers. Arthur's first experience of war was rather wet. Heavy rains combined with enemy shelling had caused damage to the trench system and there was a continual need to carry out repairs. During this tour the cooking system changed. No cooking was allowed in the trenches and cooked food was brought forward - cooking smoke was a good point of aim for enemy gunners!

Following a six mile march, the men arrived at Leal Villiers where they were housed in billets. A complete day was spent cleaning and then there were company parades and route marches for a few days, Arthur had no time to sit and dwell about the awful conditions of trench life.

The rest of 1915 was spent rotating between the front lines, at the rear resting and moving forward as a reserve unit where the days were spent on working parties repairing and improving trenches. The main dangers were from shelling and snipers, on one occasion an incident happened at night in the front line which reminded the men to be vigilant at all times. A lone German soldier managed to infiltrate a trench and shot two sentries, one man five times, and after a scuffle where he stabbed another sentry in the back he managed to make good his escape leaving behind his cap.

Christmas 1915 found Arthur out of the trenches at Varennes and the day was treated as a holiday with bath parades held in the morning. On Boxing Day, the Battalion went back into the line at Mailly-Maillett. The changeover was quiet but one man was killed in the process. The next few days were spent keeping heads down from artillery and sniper fire until they were relieved on 29th December and marched to Acheux where they cleaned, rested and were entertained by the Follies. At the beginning of the war entertainment was organised on a Battalion basis with volunteers presenting music hall type entertainment with sing songs and drag artists to add a touch of female flavour. As the war progressed this was then organised at a divisional level and on a semi-professional basis with the various Folly troupes giving themselves catchy names, the

16th Battalion of the Royal Warwickshire Regiment formed a Folly called the 'Brum Boys'.

At the beginning of February, the companies were cleaned and issued with new clothing one day at a time. There then commenced an extensive training programme lasting until the end of February; PT, rifle and bayonet drills, route marches, musketry on the rifle range, including quick reloads, to achieve the rapid fire standard of 15 rounds per minute. Specialist training was provided for the Lewis Gunners and communication skills for the subalterns (2nd Lieutenants). However, the last proper bath that the men had enjoyed had been on the11th January when the Battalion had marched from Forceville to Acheux specifically for that purpose. This bath had to last until 27th March 1915, when again whilst in reserve the Battalion were afforded the luxury of a good hot bath. In these lengthy periods between baths, the men were continually in a state of wet from rain, snow or mud and had to make best use of any facilities available to clean themselves, their uniforms and equipment, whilst not in the front line trenches.

The routine of trench life was broken on 17th April 1916, when at 4p.m., a raid on an opposing German trench was mounted by two officers and 25 men, the whole Battalion was on standby for this. The raid was planned for the men to approach the trench under cover of an artillery bombardment and for the party to split into three groups, one left one right and the third to remain in situ and defend the exit point at all costs. The intention of the raid was to take prisoners, equipment and intelligence. This was achieved without any serious injury and the raid deemed a tremendous success, resulting in a congratulatory note from the brigade commander. Numerous bombs were thrown into dugouts creating an unknown number of casualties and valuable intelligence gathered with regards to the construction of the enemy trench and its defences.

May and most of June 1916, was spent in training, with particular emphasis on practise attacks on enemy trenches. On18[th]June, the Battalion took over trenches at Auchonvillers in preparation for their involvement in the great offensive of the Battle of the Somme, simply called at the time 'The Great Push'. On 24[th]June, the five day bombardment (later changed to seven) started in preparation for the infantry assault. The following afternoon, gas was released by a specialist party of the 1st Battalion, the wind changed direction and one of the gas cylinders leaked after being hit by a shrapnel fragment, the result was the gas floated back to allied lines causing 16 hospitalisations and the gas attack was abandoned. German retaliatory shelling was heavy and caused large casualties during this spell in the front line. On 26th June the Battalion marched out of the front line to rest at Bertrancourt until 30th June when having rested washed and been kitted out with full attack equipment the men were then marched to assembly trenches to the rear of the Royal Irish Fusiliers, finally getting into position at 11.30pm. The strength of the Battalion at this point was 33 officers and 843 other ranks.

After a few days waiting in their designated assembly location, the Battalion was moved up to the front line. The month was then spent holding the line or in relief at camps near to Mailly-Maillet. By the end of July and rather uniquely for this particular month, the Battalion's strength actually increased to 39 officers and 855 other ranks. There were the usual extractions and additions from the strength with hospitalisation but out of the ordinary extractions were, one other rank wounded but it was judged to be self-inflicted, two other ranks returned to base as they were under age and one other rank sent to prison. Towards the end of July, the Battalion was moved by means of road march and train to the Ypres area and took up trench duties at La Brique and the Canal Bank. This same system of manning the front line and relief to rest areas continued through August and September 1916. It was rather a quiet period, with most of the duties being in trench maintenance carried out at night under the cover of darkness.

By 1st October 1916 the 1st Royal Warwickshire Regiment was back in the area of the Somme at Daours near to Amiens where they were in billets and undergoing training at Brigade level practising attacks on enemy positions in preparation for their part in the Battle of Le Transloy. The Battalion's establishment at this stage was 30 officers and 945 other ranks. They were billeted in tented accommodation which was rather uncomfortable as it was very wet. The heavy rain was causing delays in the exercises and marches being made were lengthy due to heavy traffic on the roads.

On 9th October 1916 the Battalion took over trenches east of Les Boeufs from the London Rifle Brigade. The land in front of them was to be attacked as part of a Brigade offensive; their primary objective was the brown line and the secondary objective the green line, which if held would push the British front line to the outskirts of Le Transloy at the cemetery circle. Arthur was by now a Lance Corporal and acting Corporal whilst George was a signaller.

An artillery barrage was commenced on the German positions to which they retaliated with their own artillery. The various Battalions involved in this attack were tightly packed into trenches in anticipation of the attack starting and heavy casualties were experienced due to the overcrowding in the trenches.

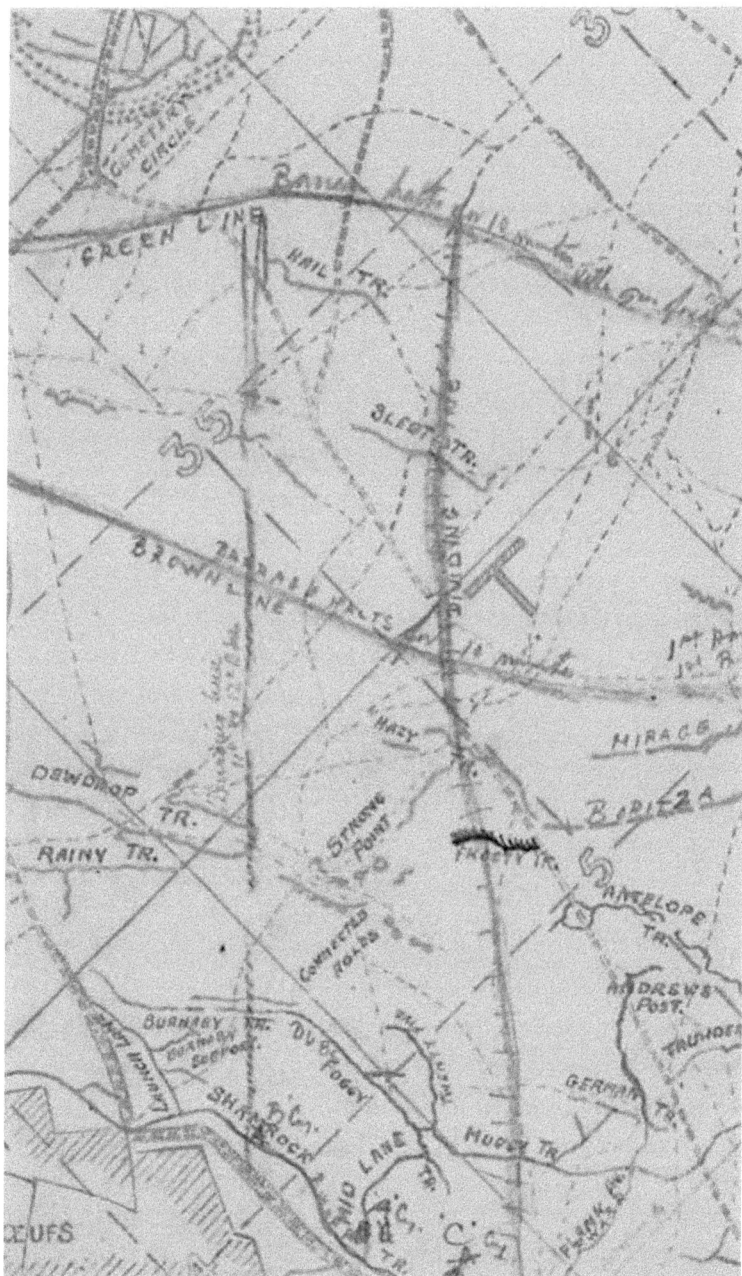

Le Transloy Trench Map, Author's collection

At 2.05 p.m. on the 12th October 1916, artillery units commenced a creeping barrage. The initial target for the artillery was in front of the first German positions for one minute then it crept forward in 25 yard steps at a rate of 50 yards per minute, when it reached the German lines it was to maintain fire on those positions for 20 minutes. Officer's whistles were blown and the 1st Battalion doubled out of the relative safety of their trenches towards their first objective, the Brown Line. Initially progress was good and reports came in of German soldiers fleeing the battle. The Battalion was moving forward on a 600 yard front, two companies wide and two companies deep. At 2.55p.m.,the companies on the left came under heavy machine gun fire from the gun pits of a German strong point; the Germans also commenced an artillery barrage on the advancing troops. Communication lines were broken and the command had to rely on returning wounded soldiers for updates. The creeping barrage ceased to be effective as it moved further forward than the advancing troops who had become pinned down by machine gun fire. All they could do was consolidate and hold the positions they were in and wait to be relieved. That relief arrived in the evening of 13th October and by 10.30 p.m. the survivors of 1st Battalion were making to the rear to clean, rest and grieve or give thanks to have survived. Arthur Owen and George Turner were among those survivors, but during this attack many of their friends did not. The casualty numbers from 9th to 13th October 1916 were; five officers and 60 other ranks killed; one officer and 158 other ranks wounded; 34 other ranks were also recorded as missing. On 22nd October 1916, orders were received to return to their former positions to resume their part in this battle.

During the evening of 22nd, the Battalion moved back to Shamrock and Fluff trenches and were in position ready for the signal to attack by 1a.m. on 23rd October. At 10.30a.m., a message was received that the start time for the attack, zero hour, had been postponed until 2.30 p.m. that afternoon, after a night sitting in a wet trench in anticipation of the forthcoming battle this message was met with mixed emotions; to some it was a stay of execution, for others an extension of a particularly uncomfortable and worrying time. The Germans knew what was coming as they had reconnaissance aeroplanes flying above the overcrowded Allied trenches. Zero hour arrived and at 2.30p.m. the attack commenced, the objectives were again the brown line and then the green line, the Battalion advanced in the same fashion as before, at the double behind a creeping barrage with the intention of the first wave capturing the first objective and consolidating that and the second wave moving on to capture the second objective and consolidating that against counter attack. Again messages were returned to the command by wounded soldiers and, needless to say, there was a steady flow of messages being sent to the rear all day. At 7.30 p.m. a message was received by the officer commanding D company that he held the strong point which had been cleared of all German troops, but he only had 14 men left. By midnight the Battalion held the strong point, Frosty and Antelope trenches, the Germans still had some positions in Hazy trench, the attack halted here but the fighting continued throughout the night and the following day.

At 2a.m. on 25th October 1916, the Battalion was relieved in the positions that they held and the survivors again made their way to the rear. On this occasion Arthur Owen and George Turner were not amongst them, having been killed in action during this second phase of the battle. Along with Arthur and George, two officers were killed and six wounded, 150 other ranks were killed, wounded or missing. The Battalion's establishment on 26th October was counted as 15 officers and 604 other ranks, they had started the month with 30 officers and 905 other ranks.

Both Arthur and George's deaths were recorded as 23rd October, the first day of this second attack and their remains were not identified. Due to this they have no known grave but could lie in a grave simply marked, 'A soldier of the Great War'. Their names are engraved along with all 1st Battalion Royal Warwickshire Regiment men who fell during the course of the battle of the Somme and have no known grave, upon Pier and Face 9 A 9 B and 10 B of the Thiepval Memorial.

Arthur left a grand sum of £1.4s.10p to his sole legatee, his mother Mary, who was also granted a war gratuity of £9. He was posthumously awarded the 1914-15 Star, British War and Victory Medals. George left a total of £5.1s.5d to his father Frederick, which was later supplemented with a War Gratuity of £6 (Indicating approximately one year and two month's service). He was posthumously awarded the British War and Victory Medals.

The Battle of Le Transloy was never deemed to be a success and was officially over by 18th October, but the fighting in this area continued as part of the greater battle of the Somme. The weather was a major factor for the Allies who were advancing over wet and boggy ground, making the reinforcement and resupply of the front line difficult, whereas the Germans were covering this ground with well aimed and positioned artillery and machine guns. The casualty figures are colossal and reach into hundreds of thousands for both sides, but this was the last action fought by the British 4th army in the Battle of the Somme which officially concluded on 18th November 1916.

Chapter 19

Frank Depperriaz Perry

On 18th November 1883, Joseph and Eugenie Perry took their baby son, Frank, to Shuttington Parish Church for his Baptism. Frank had been born in 1883 but the exact date is not recorded. Sometime between this record of Frank's birth and the 1891 Census, Eugenie Perry passed away and Joseph took his family to live at 5, Shuttington Road, Shuttington, Tamworth, the home of Mary Ann Perry who was a 65 year old Widow and Joseph's mother. The record shows three boys at this address aged five, six and seven, Frank being the middle child. The family are still living in Shuttington in 1901. Mary Perry as head of the household, is now 75 and Joseph at 44, is employed as a Hewer in the coal mine industry. Joseph's three sons have all left school and are employed as farm labourers and the youngest at 14, a milk seller.

On 6thFebruary 1909, Frank married Hetty Shepherd at Seckington Parish Church and made their home at 7, Catherine Place, Amington. At the time of the wedding, both Frank and Hetty were residents of Shuttington and Frank was working Pooley Hall Colliery as a Hewer. The couple were blessed with three children; Joseph Depperriaz, born in 1909, Blanch Eugenie, born in 1911 and Gladys, born in 1915, all in Tamworth.

Whilst Frank's military file has not survived, there is sufficient detail to state that Frank joined the Army before the commencement of World War I and served as a reservist. He was called to arms and Private 7163 Perry joined his unit, 2nd Battalion South Staffordshire Regiment, when they mobilised to France, disembarking at Le Havre of 12th August 1914. By November 1914 the initial thrust of the German invasion of Belgium and France had been halted by the British Expeditionary Force (BEF) and the French Army. The siege nature of the Western Front then formed and remained the nature of warfare for the rest of World War I with both sides launching massive offensives to break what appeared to be a stalemate. There was no specific dedicated unit which operated in tunnelling at the start of the war, but many of the engineering units had received instruction in the ancient art of tunnelling warfare. It became clear, to both sides, at an early stage that this tactic would be useful in this static type of warfare and, on 20th December 1914, ten small mines of approximately 50 Kg of, high explosive, were detonated beneath British positions at Givenchy, from Saps in the German front line. Over 800 men of the Indian Corps were lost proving the worth of tunnelling underneath the enemy positions and initiating quantities of high explosive and destroying the men and positions above.

The British responded in kind and formed a unit of men who had formerly been employed as 'Clay Kickers' in the London Underground and on 17th February 1915 the first British mine was exploded beneath Hill 60 South of Ypres by troops of the Royal Engineers (RE). Following this success, it was determined to form special tunnelling units and with men drawn from such backgrounds of sewerage works and mining, one of the first units was formed in February 1915. Frank was selected to join this unit; the 170th Tunnelling Company of the Royal Engineers (RE) and became Sapper 86543 Perry RE.

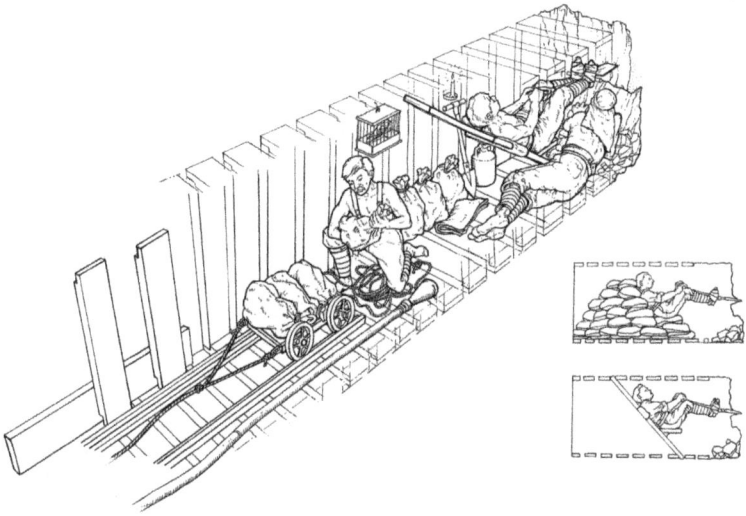

'Illustration: © Andy Gammon, andygammon.net'
Tunneller's at the face assisted by a Tunneller's mate removing spoil by means of a rail and cart system.

By April 25th 1915, the 170th Tunnelling Company RE was sufficiently formed to commence work and start a diary record of their activities. The Company was commanded by a Captain Preedy of the RE and maintained a complement constituted of officers and other ranks of the RE, plus men like Frank who because of their specialist skills were transferred from their Regiments to the RE. Wherever the Company was working, any additional labour requirements were drawn from nearby Battalions in reserve lines nearby. Later the need was seen for permanent staff and the establishment of the Companies became permanent.

In early June, Frank's father died and he was allowed home on a short leave to attend the funeral, now Frank's wife and children were living at 2, The Green, Amington, Tamworth.

Tunnelling was an extremely hazardous occupation and often the warfare above ground was also occurring below ground. Listening posts were formed and men sat in them for the sole purpose of detecting enemy mining activity. Often the tunnels would coincide and vicious hand to hand fighting would occur below ground. When enemy activity was detected, explosives would be placed in such a position that the enemy tunnel and its occupants were destroyed, the enemy were doing the same and casualties whilst mining were a regular occurrence.

South east British tunnels, North West German tunnels
Authors collection.

The above sketch shows how complex the underground works became. Each sap, which was the mouth of the tunnel, would be the access point for several different branches which could also be inter-connected and contained galleries where listening posts could be manned, stores for equipment and gathering points for the men. At the end of the tunnel a gallery was formed to contain the explosives which would be fired at a planned time, the firing of the mine could be for both offensive and defensive reasons. Offensive mines, could be placed below enemy positions to blow the position and its inhabitants above at the commencement of an attack, or they could be blown in front of enemy positions and then the resulting hole attacked and occupied thereby forming an advantageous position in front of the enemy line. In either case, it was planned that infantry would quickly follow the explosion to occupy and consolidate the position. Defensively, the mines could be blown in the event of an enemy attack or to destroy enemy underground operations.

Sometimes the enemy could be persuaded to man their positions and then mines fired beneath them. On 24th June 1915, a small charge was fired in a crater in front of German positions, at the same time the infantry commenced rapid firing and artillery started a bombardment, the Germans anticipating an infantry attack, manned their positions in the front line and then a mine containing 2,000 lbs was fired underneath them. The damage reported was considerable and no doubt inflicted large numbers of casualties on the enemy.

Gas and foul air was a constant menace to miners as it was heavier than air and would concentrate in the lowest positions it could find. Men like Frank from mining backgrounds were aware of these dangers and kept a constant watch on the situation. The flame of a candle would burn bright yellow in oxygen but turn blue in dangerous conditions. In the early days of these operations prevention was a continuing learning curve reacting to incidents which usually resulted in the death of men.

At 11 p.m., 13th August 1915, the Germans blew a mine next to a branch gallery in a tunnel being worked from Sap No. seven, this resulted in the burial of a Captain and six other ranks. A rescue mission was immediately mounted but after digging through the night it was only bodies that were recovered. On 20th August 1915, at 11.30 a.m., the Germans exploded another mine next to the end of a new gallery being constructed by Frank and his comrades, four men were killed instantly, including Frank, and one other man was wounded. Again, the rescuers recovered the bodies of the dead men but on this occasion a retaliatory charge was fired in the hope of killing any Germans working in the vicinity.

Frank was buried in grave B14 at Cambrin Military Cemetery along with two of the men killed with him, Sapper 79911 H. Jee and Sapper 86535 M Howell; a single cross headstone commemorates the three men. Under normal circumstances each dead soldier would be buried in his own grave and marked accordingly if his identity was known. In the case of an unidentified soldier or body part, the grave is simply marked, 'A Soldier Known unto God'. It is likely that in this case, the three bodies were collectively identifiable but individually not, hence the shared but marked grave. Frank lies next to Sapper 86565 F.J. Webster who was killed in the explosion on 13thAugust. Sapper Webster was from the village of Wood End near to Tamworth and no doubt known to Frank.

Frank's wife was informed of his death by telegram and she also received letters from a friend of his, Sapper Swann, who informed her of the details of her husband's death and reassured her that it was instantaneous and he did not suffer. These letters also described Frank as a popular man who was very much liked by all in his section. This information was of some comfort to her but three more children would grow up not knowing their dad. Frank left £25.10s.9d, supplemented by a War Gratuity of £5.10s.0d and the money was divided between his wife and children, Hetty would also have received a proportion of Frank's pay to prevent the family falling into poverty, until a war pension was paid.

Frank was awarded the 1914 Star, British War and Victory medals.

Chapter 20

George Pallett

Within the records of the Commonwealth War Graves Commission there are three casualties of this name. The family of the man subject of this story selected him whilst researching their family tree and of the three, he is the one living near Pooley Hall at the relevant time.

George was born in the third quarter of 1881 in the village of Cadeby, Leicestershire, the eldest child of Thomas, a Farm Labourer, and Alice Pallett. The family home was The Hollow, Cadeby, Market Bosworth, Leicestershire and by 1891, the family had expanded to five children; three boys and two girls.

In 1901, George, now 20, was living at Obaston near Market Bosworth, with his grandfather, Joseph Pallett, who was a General Agricultural Labourer, whilst George was working as a Waggoner on a farm. Living and working with them, also as a Waggoner, was William Dawson, another of Joseph's grandchildren and presumably a cousin of George.

In 1906, George married Florence Ellen Treadwell in Market Bosworth and set up home at Sibson Road, Atherstone. By 1911, the couple had three children, all girls, and George was still working as a Waggoner on a Farm. At some stage after 1911, George changed profession and worked at Pooley Hall Colliery, Polesworth. His experience as a Wagoner gave him many skills transferable to the mining industry, such as animal husbandry and haulage of goods by cart.

George's military file did not survive and it is not possible to ascertain when he joined the army, other than he enlisted at Coalville, Leicestershire, was posted as Private 204478 to the 1st Battalion Lincolnshire Regiment and served with that unit in France after 1st January 1916 until April 1918. At the outbreak of war the 1st Battalion of the Lincolnshire Regiment was based in Portsmouth and mobilised to France on 13th August 1914. In November 1915 they were transferred to the 62nd Brigade of the 21st Division. The Regiment retained a training Battalion based in England throughout the war. This was 3rd (Reserve) Battalion located in Grimsby and most likely the unit that George was sent to for basic training before being deployed to 1st Battalion in France.

On 21st March 1918, the German army on the Western Front launched an offensive, the first phase of which was to break the allied line at the point the BEF and French army met, drive the BEF north to the sea and destroy it there, forcing the French to request an armistice. The operation known as the Spring Offensive or Kaiserschlacht (Kaiser's Battle), continued until 18th July 1918 and was in four separate phases. The second phase, named 'Georgette', started on 9th April 1918 and was designed to break the British line where it was being held by the Portuguese Expeditionary Force and became known as The Battle of Lys. The German army had been reinforced on the Western Front by 50 Divisions released from the Eastern Front by the collapse of the Russian Empire. There was a real danger that this offensive would be successful and the BEF destroyed. Reinforcements were rushed to the front to hold the attacks at all cost, while a second formidable defensive wall was created to prevent the German army's forward momentum.

On that fateful first day of the German offensive, George's Battalion was in the front line near to Heudicourt, Somme

District. At 4 a.m., their positions were subjected to a heavy artillery bombardment including a gas attack, which placed a heavy white fog over the ground to their front. At 8 a.m., the bombardment was lifted and the gas fog started to clear; the German infantry had started their attack. George and his comrades were engaged all day in heavy fighting and subjected to murderous machinegun fire. During the day, the Battalion was reduced to fighting in separate pockets as their line was broken but they were reinforced by South African troops and managed to hold on and beat back the enemy. They held their ground until relieved at 3 a.m. the following day. The Battalion diary from 1st to 21st March 1918, fell into the hands of the enemy that day and unfortunately the account written later does not detail casualties. The remaining days of March were spent putting together scratch Companies along with other units to form Battalions to reinforce points along the line where weaknesses occurred.

On 1st April 1918, the depleted Battalion was entrained to Pezelhoek, Pas-de-Calais, for deployment in that sector. During the night of April 12th 1918, 10th Battalion was sent into the front line in the Wytschaete sector, near to Ypres, Belgium.

German advances from 9th to 15th April 1918.
Picture public domain via Wikipedia

The trenches had a lack of shelter and the men were subjected to a continuous and heavy artillery bombardment lasting until 16th April 1918, when the Germans launched an infantry attack. During this stage the Battalion's casualties were two officers and 80 other ranks. At 4.30 a.m., on 16th April, the intensity of the bombardment increased on the British front line for one hour. During this bombardment, George was killed and any remains, if they existed, were never identified. The German infantry then attacked, under cover of a dense fog, targeting both flanks of the depleted Battalion. The fighting was vicious and hand to hand, the dense fog making the situation confusing and denying the effective use of the Lewis Guns and rifles. This situation continued until 6.30 a.m. and the survivors then retired, carrying some of the wounded and fighting as they went. This retiring action secured the Battalion's flanks and held up the German attack until reinforcements relieved them; they then held the line until relieved on 17th April 1918.

The Battalion now consisted of five officers and 82 other ranks, they were joined the following day by 21 stragglers who had become detached in the fighting and joined up with other units. Before the first stage of the German Offensive, the Battalion's strength had been 38 officers and 935 other ranks; these two engagements had reduced the Battalion to a total of 108 men.

George, was posted missing in action and left £11.12s.10d which was supplemented with a War Gratuity of £5 (indicating a joining date early in 1917), to his wife, Florence, who would have received a part of her husband's pay until it was ascertained he was presumed dead and then a widow's pension was paid to prevent the family falling into poverty. George was awarded the British War and Victory Medals and his name was engraved on the Tyne Cot Memorial, West-Vlaanderen Belgium.

Chapter 21

Jack William Prince

Jack Prince was a volunteer to the British Army and joined the Grenadier Guards Regiment between 23rd April 1915, and 1st June 1915. These are the known dates for two soldiers who joined before and after him whose numbers are before and after Jack's. Jack was born on 10th June 1897 and therefore joined up before his 18th birthday in 1915, as conscription was not commenced until 1916, we can definitively state he was a volunteer.

Jack's parents were John Charles and Sarah Emma Prince, who in 1901 lived at 31, The Lynch, Polesworth. Jack was a miner employed as an underground horse keeper and besides Jack, they had two daughters. By 1911, Jack at 13 is employed as an underground assistant horse keeper at Pooley Hall Colliery. His father is still working in the same capacity and presumably Jack left school at 12 and went with his father to work in the mines. The family, now resident a few doors from their 1901 address at 39, The Lynch, records that a total of seven children were born to the couple alive, but two of them had since died; not unusual for the child mortality rates of the day. On 8th November 1917, Jack married Clara Eversham by special licence and the couple moved into number 33, The Lynch, Polesworth.

The lack of documentary evidence means we cannot place Jack with the 4th Battalion until 1916, (the war diaries rarely mention the other ranks by name unlike the officers), but as the 4th were in France, when we know he volunteered and joined up, he must have completed his training with a Battalion based in the UK. By March 1918, Jack, Guardsman 23825, had been promoted to Lance Corporal, no mean feat in such a prestigious Regiment as the Grenadier Guards. He was clearly a man who was dedicated to being a soldier and who was deemed to have sufficient character and control as to take command of his friends. This would indicate he had been with the 4th for sufficient time to impress his leaders that he had the potential for NCO rank.

In 1918, the Germans launched their last offensive of the war, known as the Kaiserschlacht or Ludendorff Offensive. It began on 21st March 1918 and progressed on four separate fronts. The infantry assault was preceded by a five-hour artillery bombardment in which 1,000,000 shells were fired which equates to 3000 shells per minute. The infantry attack was spearheaded by elite troops known as Stormtroopers; these men were lightly equipped and armed with such hard hitting weapons as Flamethrowers (*Flammenwerfers*). The tactic was to attack each target with speed and move quickly on to the next target, they were then followed by ordinary infantry who took prisoners and consolidated captured positions. On the first day, 21,000 British soldiers were taken prisoner, huge territorial gains were made through the area held by the British 5th Army and the high command lost control of the situation. Very soon, fresh forces were needed to be brought to that area of the front to stem the German advance and plug the gaps to stabilise the situation.

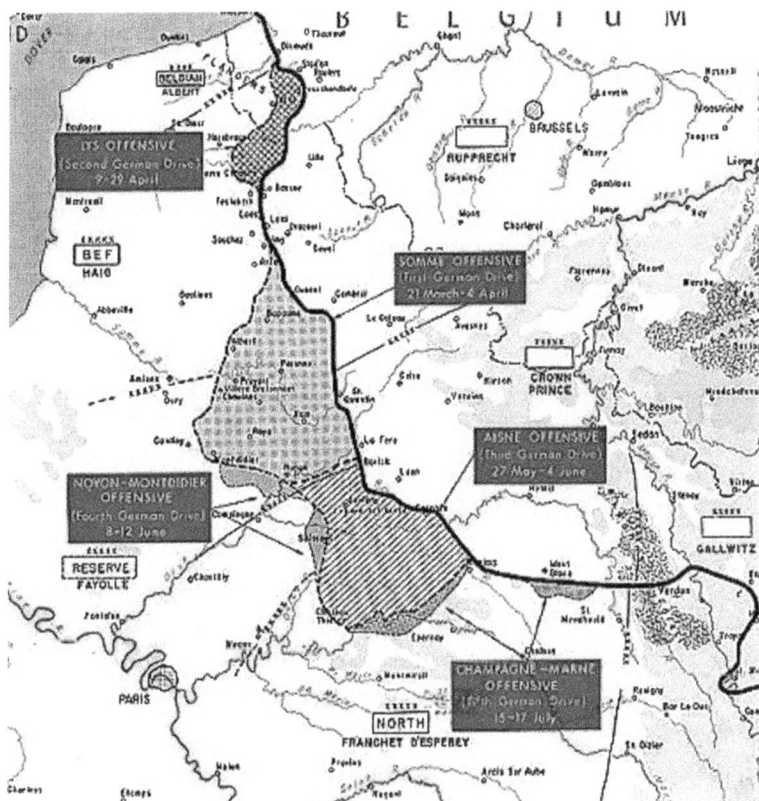

Map showing the areas of the attack and the gains
Picture public domain

One such unit to be mobilised, was Jack's 4th Battalion Grenadier
Guards which on this first day of the offensive was based at
Béthencourt, east of Arras. The Battalion was training and
heard the German bombardment commence in the distance. At
11.50 p.m., orders were received for an immediate mobilisation;
the situation was urgent from the very beginning.

The first stage of the offensive, codenamed *'Michael'*, was
designed to break the British lines, encircle and crush the armies
from behind and force the French to request an Armistice. The
three other stages of the offensive, codenamed *'Georgette'*,

'*Gneisenau*' and '*Blücher-Yorck*' were ancillary to stage one and designed to divert forces away from the main thrust of '*Michael*'. It was to the area of operations of stage two, '*Georgette*', that the 4th Battalion were directed and, on 10th April 1918, the German army attacked the British and Portuguese line south of Armentières, in overwhelming force. By nightfall of 11th April 1918, the British forces had been pushed back 10 miles and there was a real danger that the following day the Germans would take the strategically important town of Hazebrouck.

British reinforcements were being sent in from all directions and the 4th Guards Brigade, consisting of Jack's 4th Battalion, the 3rd Coldstream Guards and 3rd Irish Guards, arrived in the town of Strazele, east of Hazebrouck by motor buses, at 9.30 p.m., 11th April 1918. On arrival, the men were cold, stiff and tired, the previous night they had slept at the roadside awaiting the buses which arrived late and then spent ten hours crammed in the vehicles being transported to their destination. After a short rest and a meal, the Brigade moved off in the direction of the enemy, guided by the explosions of artillery shells. Each man carried not only his weapons and equipment but also a shovel. This last item was a very essential tool in battle situations. It was all very well capturing or falling back to positions which had been ravaged by shellfire, but it was also essential to consolidate that position and ensure it could be defended against attack. The shovel not only deepened, or even created, the position but it was used to create a step from which to fire. By dawn, the 4th Battalion was holding an extended front of two and a half miles with the Coldstream Guards on their right and the Irish Guards in reserve, a thin red line for sure!

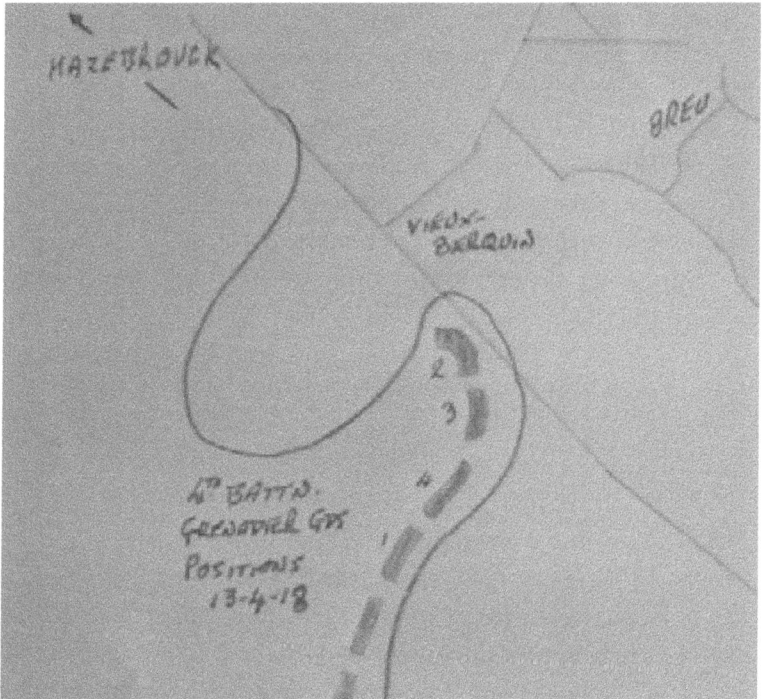

Defensive positions of 4th Battalion
Picture author's collection

At first light, 12th April 1918, the Germans continued their advance and commenced firing with field guns, rifles and machineguns. The German objective was the Forest of Nieppe, 1800 yards to their fore, from where they would have a covered approach all the way to Hazebrouck. Jack and his comrades' orders were simple; hold at all costs to the last man and bullet. The scattered line of Guardsmen commenced an accurate and devastating fire with rifles and machineguns and drove the German infantry back. The Germans then pressed a second attack, supported by Field Guns at almost point blank range, these guns had been worked up to within 300 yards of the British line under the cover of hedgerows, this second attack was repulsed but at a heavy cost. It was decided to launch a counter attack and two Companies of the Irish Guard reserve was placed onto the right of the front line and all three Battalions attacked at 11 a.m., 12th April 1918. The attack was met with heavy opposition and large numbers of casualties were experienced, but the main objective had been a delaying tactic and this was successful and gained a few precious hours. The best gains of this attack were in the area of Jack's Battalion and the hamlet of Pont Rondin was captured by No.2 Company. The attack was pressed with rifle fire and rifle grenade and 30 Germans killed, two machineguns and two prisoners taken; seven of the Germans were killed by the Company Commander, Captain Pryce.

At 3p.m.,12th April 1918, the Germans launched a third attack along the whole of the Guards Brigade's line and were in danger of succeeding apart from an unauthorized counter attack which managed to stabilize the situation. Just before dusk, the Germans launched a fourth attack, assisted by artillery, trench mortar and machinegun fire. Despite further heavy losses, the Guards drove the Germans back to their own lines. Darkness on 12th April 1918, brought no respite. Although reinforcements were on the way, the Guardsmen were still holding their positions regardless of cost. A disaster occurred to Jack's No.1 Company when all the rations and supplies were hit by artillery fire, whilst more ammunition was obtained the men received no further rations of food or water. To their rear the 1st Australian Division was busy developing an impenetrable defensive line, which when ready, but not until the night of the 13th April, would defeat the German advance and give the surviving Guards somewhere to retire to. It is no exaggeration to state that the immediate future of the British Army was in the hands of a dwindling number of extremely brave, but fatigued and bloodied men, including Lance Corporal Jack William Prince! The night was spent readjusting the line, improving defences and replenishing ammunition ready for the onslaught expected at first light.

As the dawn on 13th April 1918 broke, the British soldiers saw to their dismay a heavy fog had descended in front of them thus enabling the Germans to creep forward under its cover and place light machine guns between the scattered British posts. Attack after attack was driven back by the Guardsmen and in one location, Guardsman Jacotin of 3rd Battalion Coldstream Guards, found himself the last man alive in his post and he continued to fight and drive the Germans back until he was killed by a German who had managed to infiltrate his rear and throw a hand grenade into his position. At 12 noon, No.2 Company, under the command of Captain Pryce and holding the village of La Couronne, were subjected to a ferocious German attack which infiltrated the Village and surrounded the surviving defenders. At 6.15 p.m., 13th April, Captain Pryce and the 18 men left standing, with no ammunition left decided to sacrifice themselves and fixing bayonets charged the Germans surrounding them. The Germans found themselves unable to fire as their own comrades were in the way, the charge was successful and followed up with a second attack, the Germans were receiving reinforcements and eventually the Guardsmen were all cut down. The last man to die was Captain Pryce himself, he was last seen fighting hand to hand with overwhelming odds, this story was related by a wounded Corporal who managed to get himself to the Australian lines the following night.

The sacrifice made by the 4th Guards Brigade allowed the Australian forces to complete their defensive line and stop the German advance, this second phase of the Spring Offensive failed. Captain Pryce, who had previously been awarded the Military Cross and a bar for bravery, was posthumously awarded the Victoria Cross by King George V. Only 14 of the 120 men of No. 2 Company survived; all were wounded, POW's or both. Jack Prince paid the ultimate sacrifice and was killed in action on the last day of the battle, 13th April 1918. His company had been subjected to continuous machine gun fire all day, but had continued to fight no matter how heavy the casualty toll had become. The only surviving officer of Jack's No. 1 Company, Captain Minchin, himself shot three times, returned to British lines with the six men of his company who were not killed or wounded. The survivors of the 4th Guards Brigade retired to the Australian lines and started taking stock of the toll these few days had taken on their number, however, they had not finished fighting as they remained, manning the front line for another day until ordered to the rear. 90% of the 4th Battalion were casualties, 504 men either killed or wounded.

The casualty lists initially posted many of the men as missing, including Jack, but when the battlefield was eventually cleared, his body was recovered, identified and he was buried in Aval Wood Military Cemetery at Viex-Berquin France. Jack left £13.8s1d. supplemented by a War Gratuity of £13 to his wife, Clara and he was awarded the British War and Victory Medals.

Chapter 22

Charles Edward Riley

There is very little known about Charles but this does not make him any less worthy of mention than if there was an abundance of information. The main reasons for this situation are his extremely youthful demise and the loss of his military record.

Charles was born on 10th January 1901, in Polesworth, Warwickshire. His mother was Maria Riley of Yarrows Yard, Market Street. His father is recorded as unknown.

At some stage, probably when he was 12, he became employed at the Pooley Colliery and some time prior to November 1917 he enlisted in the British army and was assigned for training to the Devonshire Regiment, as Private TR8/94111. The number issued to Charles shows he was in training and the most likely Battalion he was posted to was 3rd (Reserve). This unit was raised in August 1914 and remained in the UK throughout the war. At the time Charles served, the Battalion had moved to Plymouth and was employed in the defence of that City.

Unfortunately, the only other records that exist of poor Charles are his date and cause of death, plus the register entry of soldier's effects.

Charles died on 22nd November 1917, cause of death recorded as Spotted Fever, in an isolation hospital in Norwich and was buried in a nearby cemetery, grave reference 26.244. The register of effects shows his sum wealth to be £5.6 shillings plus a war gratuity of £3 which passed to his father Thomas Riley.

Spotted fever is worthy of an explanation as it was one of the hazards faced by soldiers and very often led to an inglorious, painful death. Whilst conscription had been in force since 1st January 1916, it only applied to men aged between 18 and 41 years of age, Charles was undoubtedly a volunteer. He had answered the call to arms at the age of 16 and may well have been less than honest about that fact. Following the carnage of the first two years of the war and in particular, the recent offensive on the Somme, the recruiting staff was probably not asking too many questions! He had no doubt joined for reasons of adventure, service to King and country or to get away from home and a hard and uncertain future. By this stage in the war the public were well aware of the likelihood of injury or death, not many communities were untouched by the carnage of the previous two plus years, but a 16 year old boy with a sense of adventure and a humdrum existence would not be deterred. Charles was clearly a man of determination to achieve an objective and hard working with leadership skills. In the short time he was in the Army he had been assessed worthy of promotion to Lance Corporal. At the time of his death Charles was assigned to 210th Graduated Battalion. This was a training Battalion with no affiliation to a particular regiment but during the course of Charles's service became a unit of the Devonshire regiment and moved to Norwich from Taversham.

Spotted fever is a bacterium based infection, transmitted to humans by a tick, probably hosted by a dog. The infected ticks leave their host to feed from a human and the bacteria is spread via the bite, most likely in the spring or summer months. Charles was most likely to have been infected in the summer months prior to his death and the culprit tick was attached to him for more than 20 hours. Within days of being bitten Charles developed a fever and may have had such symptoms as chills, headaches, confusion, pain, diarrhoea and vomiting. A distinctive red spotted rash appeared on his wrists and ankles, hence the name, which then spread to the rest of his body. Reporting sick at quite an early stage of the infection was followed by a diagnosis and he was soon segregated from his comrades and then moved to the specialist hospital at Norwich. This condition still exists and is successfully treated with antibiotics which had not been discovered in 1917. Charles developed complications likely affecting his heart, kidney or lungs and his actual cause of death was shock from organ or multiple organ failure.

An ignominious death to a short life was no less a hammer blow to Charles's family, former workmates and the Polesworth community. Due to his military status Charles is honoured on the Pooley Colliery memorial his grave recorded and tended by the Commonwealth War Graves Commission and his memory kept alive by the Royal British Legion and the nation on the 11[th]hour, of the 11th day, of the 11th month.

Chapter 23

Frank Startin

Frank was born on 3rd May 1895, the second son but fifth child, of Joseph and Annie Startin of 17, John Street, Glascote, Tamworth. He was baptised on 28th May the same year. By 1901 the family had expanded to six children; two sons and four daughters whose ages ranged from two to 16 years of age. None were shown to be in employment and the lack of comment on the form about children in school would indicate that those not employed and of school age, were in school. The only person employed is Frank's father, Joseph, who has his own business as a Hawker/Fishmonger. Business must have been good to allow his children to stay in school beyond the legal limit of 12. In 1911, the family had moved to 35, John Street, Glascote and the business was being run by Frank's mother, Annie. Joseph, 56 years old, had become an invalid (as described) and unable to work. Annie, 55 years old and 27 years married to Joseph, had delivered seven live babies of which five had survived to this date. Frank at 15, was working below ground at Pooley Hall Colliery as a Pony Driver, his scholarly opportunities cut short by his father's invalidity.

Following the outbreak of World War I, Frank volunteered along with the thousands of other men who answered the call to arms, and was enlisted into the North Staffordshire Regiment, 1/6 Battalion, which had been raised in August 1914, at Burton-on-Trent. Private 1948 Startin completed basic training and mobilised to France with his Battalion, landing at Le Havre on 5th March 1915, having embarked from Southampton the previous day on board the SS Empress Queen. This places him in either A or B Company who, with the HQ staff, formed the second half of the Battalion to sail from Southampton; the first half having sailed the previous day on the SS Balmoral.

From 21st to 24th March 1915, the Battalion received instruction in trench warfare following which they marched to Bailleul where they were billeted in Aldershot Camp awaiting their turn to go into the front line. On April 5th 1915, they relieved the 1/5 Battalion, North Staffordshire Regiment, in trenches near to Wulverghem. They were relieved on the evening of 9th April and in those first few days three men were killed, one wounded and one man missing, probably as a result of enemy shelling on their positions.

On 1st day of the Battle of the Somme, 1st July 1916, Frank's Battalion was part of an Assault on Gommecourt Wood and Village. Their attack commenced at 7.30 a.m., preceded by an artillery barrage of 65 minutes, the men left their trenches and attacked under cover of a smoke screen. As experienced elsewhere on the Somme the expectations of the artillery bombardment of the preceding seven days were not realised and various things went wrong. The enemy and their positions were not destroyed and they very quickly manned the parapets and laid down a devastating enfilade with machine guns and rifles. The Germans were prepared for the infantry assault and also used artillery to great effect by targeting the centre ground of the advance with both high explosive and shrapnel shells. The attackers had objectives where the wire had been cut but many were lost in the smoke and did not reach these locations, they were then at the mercy of the machine gunners and artillery. It had rained heavily prior to the attack and conditions were very difficult to advance through, with thick mud to overcome. At 5 p.m., the survivors of the Battalion were relieved and retired to billets. The casualties for the day were; eight officers killed, six wounded, and four missing with 34 other ranks killed, 170 wounded and 122 missing: a total of 344 men.

The Battalion went into reserve and for the next few months did not take part in specific attacks but went into the usual rotation of front line, support and reserve. At the start of September 1916, the Battalion took up positions in the front line near to Ransart, south-west of the city of Arras. The periods were, 28th August to 3rd September, 9th to 15th September and 21st to 27th September. During one of these tours in the front line, Frank was hit by a sniper's bullet, the bullet hit him in the chest area and passed through both of his lungs but he wasn't killed outright. Frank was taken to the nearby aid post and from there to a casualty clearing station, where doctors fought to save his life. He was visited by the Brigade Chaplain who later wrote to Frank's family telling them that he bore his sufferings like a man and it was thought he may pull through but unfortunately, Frank's strength failed him and he subdued to the grievous wound and died on 28th September 1916.

Frank was buried nearby in De Cusine Ravine British Cemetery, Basseux, and the ceremony was officiated by the Brigade Chaplain. Many of Frank's friends were able to attend the funeral as they had been relieved from the front line the day before he died. Frank left £2.12s.3d which was added to with a War Gratuity of £9 to his mother Susan and he was awarded the 1914-15 Star, British War and Victory Medals.

Chapter 24

Oliver Charles Storer

Oliver was born in the year 1897. There is no record of his birth or Christening available. Exact birthdates from this era are usually found in records of Christenings which also had a place for the 'alleged birth date' to be recorded. His parents, Ambrose Storer-a Sanitary Pipe Burner -and his mother, Annie, had made a family home at 20, East View, Glascote, Tamworth. Oliver was the seventh child for Annie who in total bore ten children eight of whom lived until 1911 when at that census the family address is recorded as 35, Lynch, Polesworth. Oliver, now 14 years old, has left school and is working as a Coal Sorter, a job on the surface.

In February 1915, the year of his eighteenth birthday, Oliver enlisted at Atherstone and was posted to the Royal Warwickshire Regiment. His only surviving military records show he served with 2nd Battalion, but a newspaper article reporting the circumstances of his death state that on joining he went to the Isle of Wight and from there to France, in February 1916. The

2nd Battalion, a Regular unit of the British Army, was mobilised to France in October 1914, but the 3rd (Reserve) Battalion was a training unit and during the relevant period was based on the Isle of Wight. If the dates given in the newspaper article are correct, then Oliver was in training for a year. It may well be that he joined before being eighteen and could not go abroad until after his birthday. This is even more likely, as when he joined he was accepted for home defence but then elected to sign up for active service abroad. It gives us a picture of a young man eager to serve his country in any capacity but, at the earliest opportunity, elected to get into the war to do his bit.

Reinforcements arrived on three days of February 1916; 11th, 28th and 29th. Whichever of those days Oliver arrived with his new Battalion, it was wet and he joined them in the trenches forward of Morlancourt in the Somme district just below Albert. During the next few months, Oliver became used to the routine of rotating between holding the front line, being in reserve and being out of the trenches at Morlancourt. This duty was producing a regular supply of casualties, both killed and wounded, the most common cause now being shrapnel wounds from exploding enemy artillery. On 30th June 1916, the Battalion paraded at Lucknow Redoubt, the assembly point for the operations they were to take part in during the initial stages of the Battle of the Somme. At 7.30 a.m. on 1st July 1916, the Battalion moved into trenches vacated by the assaulting troops in the first wave of the battle. At 2.30 p.m., they were ordered to assist in the taking of Mametz, this was achieved along with the capture of 200 prisoners, two machine guns and an automatic rifle, they then occupied trenches until relieved on the night of 5th July. The Battalion's casualties at this stage were; four officers and three other ranks killed; two officersand 98 other ranks wounded; 14 other ranks missing.

A few days were spent in a camp at Heilly and then the Battalion moved to Mametz Woods where they bivouacked, coming under artillery fire and taking casualties. On 13th July 1916, the Battalion was engaged in attacking the enemy's second line and during the day came under heavy machinegun fire. This fighting lasted until 20th July when they were relieved and proceeded to Dernacourt where they bivouacked. The casualty list from this engagement was; one officer and 219 other ranks killed, five officers and 142 other ranks wounded, with 62 other ranks missing. Oliver was severely wounded in the left arm and right leg and rushed to hospital. From here he was transported by rail and ship to England, where he was taken to Queen Mary's Military Hospital at Whalley Lancashire. Unfortunately, septic poisoning set in and he died from Tetanus on the morning of Sunday 23rd July, 1916.

On 21st July 1916, his family had received a letter informing them of Oliver's wounds and that he was in Queen Mary's Hospital. His mother Annie and one of his sisters, travelled to Lancashire to be with him and were at his bedside when he passed away. Oliver's body was transported back to Tamworth where it was met by a party from the 20th Company of the Royal Defence Corps (RDC) from Polesworth and escorted to his home. On Thursday 27th July 1916, Oliver was buried with military honours at Polesworth Parish Church. The Polesworth band was in attendance, the RDC provided a firing party, and an honour guard consisting of a Sergeant and 12 men was sent from the North Staffordshire Regiment. Oliver was later awarded the British War and Victory Medals.

Chapter 25

John Edward Such

John was born in 1885, in Warton, Tamworth, to Henry and Hannah Such. Henry Such was employed as a Bricklayer and in total Hannah produced eight children who all survived up to and until the 1911 census. By the age of 16, John had left school and was working as a Bricklayer's Labourer, no doubt mixing mortar and carrying bricks for his father. At the age of 26, John was still a single man living with his parents at Church View, Warton and had changed direction in his career and was now working as a Holer at Pooley Hall Colliery as was his elder brother, Robert.

As is usual, John's military file is not available but his medal card tells us he went to France on 21st July 1915 and records his unit as 16th Battalion Kings Royal Rifles Corps. However, the entry for John, Rifleman R2273, in the Corps register of awards shows that John was also in the 10th Battalion.

The 16th Battalion landed at Le Havre on 17th November 1915, so it is clear that when John enlisted at Atherstone he was posted to 10th Battalion KRR Corps who disembarked at Boulogne of the same day as John's record states, 21st July 1915, and later he was posted to the 16th Battalion.

In mid-May 1917, John, now a Lance Corporal, and his Battalion were in the front line at St Léger, between Arras and Bapaume. They were relieved on 15th May and marched to the rear to Moyenneville. The Battalion then spent a few days practising attacks for a forthcoming operation. The operation was an attack on the German line at Boullecourt and although the official history of the Battle of Arras shows this conflict ending on 16th May 1917, this was part of that overall action.

At 9.50 p.m. on 19th May 1917, John lined up with his Battalion, which was third in order of the Brigade attack, at the assembly point. He, like all the men, were carrying their Lee Enfield rifles, ammunition, bayonet, two Mills Bombs, haversack, waterproof sheet, two sandbags, emergency rations, one preserved ration, one flare and either a red or a white Very light. 100 pickaxes and 200 shovels were distributed amongst the Companies for the purposes of consolidating any positions captured from the enemy. At 11.40 p.m. that night they were in place and ready to go,with Zero Hour planed for 5 a.m. the following morning. The men had ample time to reflect on issues important to them, one account given by a survivor of the war to the Imperial War Museum stated that it was impossible to fully describe the feelings but that the mind was full of wild thoughts and fancies beyond control with recollections of family, friends, places visited and former experiences, only ended by the officers passing instruction to get ready.

The initial stage of the attack was by use of the element of surprise with no artillery support, the objectives were the Hindenburg and support lines to their front. At 5.03 a.m., the men left their trenches and advanced on the enemy lines. The front line was taken with little resistance. At zero hour, 5.15 a.m., the British artillery commenced a bombardment of the German support line. The German artillery replied with a barrage of their own, which was brought down on the assembly areas and their own front line now occupied by John and his comrades. This artillery duel continued throughout the day and at 10 a.m., the orders were received to attack the secondary objective; the German support trench. The attack was attempted but at 12.35 p.m. 20th May 1917, aeroplane reconnaissance reported that the objective had not been taken, patrols were sent out on foot to ascertain the situation which confirmed the aerial reports. At 7.15 p.m., with the situation the same an estimation of casualties to date was recorded as five officers and 350 other ranks, a second attempt was to be made on the support line with two fresh Battalions. The 16th Battalion KRR Corps, held its positions in the Hindenburg Front Line until 2.45 a.m. 23rd May 1917, when it was relieved and retired to billets at Moyenneville.

The final list of casualties was compiled and recorded as; two officers and 23 other ranks killed, four officers and 138 other ranks wounded, five other ranks wounded and missing, two officers and 55 other ranks missing. John was listed in the missing category but eventually recorded as presumed dead. His body was not identified and his name was subsequently added to the long list of those missing on the Arras Memorial in Bay 7, to the war memorial in his home town, Warton, and at Pooley Hall Colliery. John left £8.12s.2d. which was supplemented with a War Gratuity of £12.10s.0d. to his mother Hannah and he was awarded the 1915 Star, British War and Victory Medals.

Chapter 26

Joseph Talbott

On April 28th 1889, the Priest in Charge of Elford Parish Church, Staffordshire, Curate L. Jones, baptised Joseph Talbott, the son of John and Mercy Ann Talbott of Cottage 7, Chilcote, Tamworth. Joseph had been born that year in Fisherwick. He was the youngest of five children with three elder brothers and a sister. The father, John, was an agricultural labourer but moved to the local coal industry and as the boys became of age they followed their father into that line of work in one capacity or another. By 1901, the family have moved to 115, Main Road, Tamworth, four doors up from the police station where Constable William Goodwin and his wife Rose resided. In 1911, the family, now comprising John and Mercy Ann, Joseph, two younger brothers, his sister Ellen, and her husband, were resident at a farm on School Lane, Ammington. Joseph, still single at 22, is employed as a Filler mine worker. All the males of the Talbott family had entered the coal mining industry except Joseph's two younger brothers, one of whom works from home as a farmer and the other is a below ground Clay Miner. John, who is now a Coal Carter, and Mercy Ann have been married for 42 years and have produced 16 children born alive of whom 13 have to date survived; a good record for the times.

On 1st September 1914, Joseph attended the recruitment station for the 6th Battalion, North Staffordshire Regiment for attestation. Joseph had at some stage served with this Battalion which was a Territorial unit, but by this date he was no longer a member. Whilst all previous records show that the family were mainly involved in the Coal Industry, this military file is the first to show that Joseph was working at the Pooley Hall Colliery. His file also shows that he had married Elsie May Wright at St Editha's Church in Tamworth, on 4th August 1913 and that on 9th June 1914, his son Sidney Talbott had been born. His medical examination that day records him as 5'4½" tall with a fully inflated chest measurement of 38 inches, a full four inches showing that although he was a small man in stature but physically very fit. Joseph was enlisted to the 6[th]Battalion, North Staffordshire Regiment and given the number 2537 and further declared that he was prepared to serve anywhere in any place outside of the United Kingdom in the event of national emergency. This was relevant to the Territorial Battalions at this stage as the volunteers were given the choice, if the individual requested not to be posted for service abroad they were assigned to a Battalion destined for home service. At the outbreak of war, the War Office had instructed all Territorial Battalions to separate men who had volunteered for service abroad and for them to be assigned to First Line Battalions, whilst the Home Service units were designated Second Line Battalions. Joseph commenced his basic training with the 6[th]Battalion, North Staffordshire Regiment which had been raised in Thorp Street, Birmingham, where there was an army barracks.

On 7th November 1914, Army Order 477, instructed the formation of the Army Cyclist Corps (A.C.C.). Following this order, probably in early 1915, Joseph, being able to ride a bike, was posted to this new formation. There were in existence some cyclist units and their primary role was reconnaissance and communication. When the above order came into force, all cyclists and men in training to be cyclists were transferred to the newly formed Corps. Officers were seconded from other regiments and the pay and structure was the same as any other Infantry unit. The men were formed into Companies and each Company assigned to a Divisional Commander for deployment as they saw fit within his Division. Later in the War the A.C.C. was reorganised on a Battalion basis and given its own command structure. Joseph's file shows that his Company was transferred to A.C.C. command on 1st November 1916. The 10th Company A.C.C., which Joseph was serving with at the time of his death, was transferred to A.C.C. Command on 17th May 1916, and started its own independent war diary on that date. Certainly, by March 1915, Joseph was a member of the Cyclists Corps as, on the 7th March 1915, he attended before the commanding officer on a charge 'refusing to obey an order given by a superior officer' and was sentenced to ten days punishment but ten days of what, is indecipherable in what remains of his record. Then in May 1915, Joseph found himself again before the commanding officer on a charge of 'insolence to an NCO', on this occasion Joseph was sentenced to three days Field Punishment number one.

There were two types of field punishment, numbers one and two, the latter was a less severe measure and involved a soldier being fettered and handcuffed, but allowed free movement otherwise. Field punishment number one involved the miscreant, not only being fettered and handcuffed, but also being tied to a fixed object such as a fence post or a gun wheel for two hours per day, for three days out of every four. During the early stages of the war, the individual was often tied with legs and arms outstretched giving rise to the nickname, 'Crucifixion'. These two types of punishment had been devised following the abolition, in 1881, of flogging and could be awarded by a commanding officer for up to 28 days, whilst a court martial could give up to 90 days. During World War 1, Field Punishment number one was carried out on 60,210 occasions. If at the front line, the individual was removed to the rear.

On 28th February 1915, Joseph embarked from Southampton to France but the detail in his file at this point is vague or obliterated and the war diary for his unit is not available or non-existent. We do know he embarked from Marseille on 5th January 1916, and arrived in Alexandria on 11th February 1916. The original intention was to post his unit to Egypt but this was cancelled and Joseph returned to France.

On 1st November 1916, Joseph was transferred to the command of the Army Cyclist Corps, until this point we do not know with which unit he had been serving, as the cyclist Companies were assigned to the Divisional Commanders, but he was now assigned an A.C.C. personal number 13296. Joseph was now part of 10th Corps Cyclist Battalion who had been officially formed on 17th May 1916 whilst serving in France.

The 10th Company had recently moved from under the command of the 4th army to that of the 2ndarmy, and had endured a march to their new location near to Abele in Belgium, where Joseph joined his new unit. The war diary makes interesting comments at this stage about the problems experienced by the cyclists; whilst march discipline was described as good some soldiers did not put sufficient effort into hill climbs causing straggling. It does mention that there had been few opportunities to use the cycles during the proceeding few months due to the type of work they had been employed in, so no doubt fitness for cycling was a key issue. The bikes were old and although they stood up to the work well there was breakages of saddles and other parts due to the potholed roads they were using. One problem they were experiencing was burst tyres, the repairing of which was made more difficult if the tube contained 'Tyreoid' which was an adhesive and probably present in the tube from a previous repair. The march was undertaken with a cavalry unit and the animals were described as in poor condition at the end of the journey and in need of good food and rest. The Cyclists own animals were used to haul carts containing supplies and a food cart. This cart would go ahead with the objective of reaching fixed points in advance of the main column and, at the daily destination, to prepare tea and meals for the men when they arrived. The establishment of horses for the Company, was nine draught horses for cook's carts and limbered wagons, and four heavy draught horses for train wagons, which were used for the baggage and supplies.

The Company were used for a variety of different work details, carrying parties at night or day for the artillery and providing orderlies-presumably for senior officer staff. All officers, NCOs and selected privates were instructed to learn the layout of the area for future use as guides and in the event of any action. Cycle patrols were mounted to report on bridges and canals, these being constant targets of enemy artillery a constant watch was kept on their condition. Night work was undertaken which lasted about five hours, building up parapets and drainage in the trench system. Whilst the diary notes that the accommodation was farm buildings and very comfortable, I suspect this comment was about the officer's quarters. The men may have been lucky to have a barn but otherwise would have been under canvass; the weather was noted as wet and cold.

On 13th November 1916, the Company was moved to accommodation in Victoria Camp; Poperinghe (now spelt Poperinge). The area was used as a concentration location and contained numerous camps to accommodate men backwards and forwards to the front. This was clearly closer to the front than the previous accommodation as the working parties went out on bicycles rather than buses. Christmas day 1916 was spent in camp with no working parties; a dinner and a concert were arranged for the men in the dining hall.

During January 1917, Lewis Guns were issued to the A.C.C., two per company, along with 2,000 rounds of ammunition which had to be transported by bicycle. Up to this point the men carried their Lee Enfield rifle attached to the bicycle in either a leather rifle scabbard or in metal brackets attached to the frame of the cycle. An officer, sergeant and two other ranks were despatched to the divisional school to attend a Lewis Gun Course and, following sufficient men being trained, these weapons and their crews were used in an anti-aircraft capacity.

The next few months were routine; the time spent on working parties, traffic control and training. The only casualties experienced were from exposure to gas. Between 7th and 14th June 1917, the 2nd Army fought the battle of Messines. This was a success but involved large casualty figures on both sides. The allies lost 24,500 whilst the German army lost 25,000 men with 10,000 missing and 7,200 men taken prisoner. On 11th June, whilst the battle raged on, the 10th A.C.C. provided working parties for burial duties and salvage. Three officers and 100 men were sent to bury the dead of this conflict and one officer with 50 men was sent to salvage equipment from the battlefield. The latter was clearly the safer of the two jobs as there were no casualties reported but the burial parties suffered, four men killed, two died of wounds, nine men were wounded and one man reported missing.

On 1st July 1917, Joseph was awarded Class 1 Proficiency Pay, this was a bonus paid to cyclists who had attained a high standard of physical endurance and qualified as proficient cyclists. On 28th July Joseph submitted a hand written letter to his chain of command notifying them that a mistake had been made in the payment of this bonus as he had been entitled to it since 1st September 1916, there is no record of this matter being rectified, (this would have been a substantial amount of money as the records show it to be 1 shilling per day in 1914).

On 6th August 1917, the Company moved to a location called 'Bluff Tunnels' and there stood by with 30 minutes notice to move to the front line. Over the next few days, they provided working parties carrying stores for the Royal Engineers. They were clearly in a dangerous location as, on the 9th August, Private Pugh was killed by an exploding artillery shell and he was buried at Bus House Cemetery. This danger continued as on

12th August 1917, five men became casualties from artillery fire; three of the men were killed, one of whom was Joseph Talbott. On the morning of the 14th August the Company moved from Bluff Tunnels back to the safety of Victoria Camp. Joseph's luck had run out and he became just one number in a horrendous list which continued to lengthen for at least one more year.

The two other men killed by the same shell were also buried in Bus House Cemetery located near the village of Voormezele, Belgium (row H13) with Private Pugh. This cemetery was so named after a London bus which had broken down nearby in no man's land in 1914. Joseph's death was reported in the Tamworth Herald and reads;

> *Mrs. J. Talbott, 3 Middle Entry, Church Street, Tamworth, has been notified of the death of her husband 13296 Pte. Joseph Talbott, Cyclist Corps, who was killed in action on August 12. He was 28 years of age, and had been on service in France for two years and six months. He belonged to the Tamworth Territorials. He was formerly employed at Pooley Hall Colliery.*

Records show that Joseph left £2.7s.7d to his wife, Elsie, which was later supplemented by a War Gratuity of £14, quite a large sum in comparison to others noted in the register of soldier's effects, but represented almost three years service. On 4th March 1918, Elsie was awarded a widow's pension of 18 shillings and 9 pence per week, this replaced a separation allowance which had been paid to Elsie following Joseph's death. This allowance was a proportion of a soldiers pay to ensure that families of men who died while in service were not left destitute. No doubt the late payment of Joseph's proficiency pay affected the sum paid to Elsie.

Joseph was also awarded the 1914-15 Star, the British War and Victory Medals, also known as Pip, Squeak and Wilfred; the medals were forwarded to Elsie in 1918.

Chapter 27

Sydney Wood

In the available records relating to this name, there are two men named Sydney Wood, one from Polesworth and one from Dordon, both miners. The only very slight difference between the two, is that Sydney Wood from Polesworth lived slightly nearer to Pooley Hall Colliery than his namesake. It could also be that both men worked at Pooley Hall and by an administrative error the name was engraved only once. To avoid identifying the wrong man it is right to tell both men's stories but identify them by their village.

Sydney Wood (Polesworth)

Sydney's family were not local folk. His father, George, was from Wombourne, Staffordshire, near to Wolverhampton and his mother, Louisa, was born in Wooton, Northamptonshire. Their children were born in a variety of places which could mean either that the family moved around, or that mother went away to have her babies in confinement. In 1901, the family now consisted of six children. Sydney being the fourth of five sons and the sixth child a nephew of George, were living at New Street, Hall End, Polesworth. Sydney was born in 1892 in Shipley, Staffordshire, and baptised at Shipley Common on 24th January 1892. By 1911 the family had moved to Pooley Lodge, Polesworth and George had changed his profession from Coal Miner Hewer to Farm Labourer.

Louisa, who has by now been married to her husband for 33 years, has borne six children of whom five have survived to date. Sydney, now 19, is employed as a Coal Miner, below ground Driver and his younger brother, aged 13, is employed as a Brickyard Hand. These two boys were the only ones left at home. The elder brothers were all Coal Miners.

Neither men's military files have survived, but this Sydney joined the Leicestershire Regiment and was posted to the 6th Battalion as Private 10885. He went to France on 29th July 1915 with his Battalion and it is probable he volunteered at the outbreak of war.

Between 14th and 17th July 1916, the 6th Battalion, Leicestershire Regiment - as part of the Fourth Army - was engaged in the Battle of Bazentin Ridge during the Battle of the Somme. The objectives of the attack were the villages of Bazentin le Petit, Bazentin le Grand and Longueval which was adjacent to Delville Wood, with High Wood on the ridge beyond. Four divisions made the attack, on a front of 6,000 yards commencing at 3:25 a.m., following a five minute hurricane artillery bombardment. Field artillery fired a creeping barrage and the four attacking waves pushed up close behind it in no man's land, leaving them only a short distance to cross when the barrage lifted from the German front trench. The first German line was reached and found to be quite badly damaged but 30 prisoners were taken. The second line was reached but few Germans were in occupation. This line was also found to be damaged and difficulty was experienced repairing the damage sufficiently to consolidate the position. While crossing No Man's Land, heavy casualties were taken from enemy machine guns situated in Bazentin-le-Petit and Bazentin-le Grand Woods, these guns were eventually silenced and captured, the crews being killed. These positions were consolidated and held until 6 a.m. 15th July 1916 and then an attack was mounted on the village of Bazentin-le-Petit which was successfully taken resulting in three German officers and 200 soldiers being taken prisoner. The Battalion occupied and defended positions taken outside of the village until they were relieved on 16thJuly. During this period, they successfully defended against two counter attacks and took another 50 prisoners. The casualty count for this engagement was; seven officers killed and 20 wounded, 500 other ranks killed, wounded and missing of which Sydney Wood was one.

Sydney's body was never recovered or identified and his name was subsequently engraved on pier and face 2 C and 3 A of the Thiepval Memorial. He left £3.19s.9d. supplemented by a War Gratuity of £8.10s to his mother Louisa and he was awarded the 1914-15 Star, Victory and British War Medals.

Sydney Wood (Dordon)

Sydney Wood from Dordon, was a local man being born in that village in 1894 to Samuel and Susan Wood. Samuel was a below ground Labourer in a colliery and in 1911 the family were resident at 185, Fair View, Dordon. By this time Sydney was 17 years of age and employed as a Pony Driver in a colliery. Susan and Samuel Wood had been married for 27 years and produced nine children all of whom had survived to this date.

Following the outbreak of war, Sydney enlisted in the army at Atherstone and was posted to the 12th (Service) Battalion, King's Royal Rifle Corps and allocated the number Rifleman A/2059. This Battalion was formed in Winchester in September 1914 and moved to Bisley. It moved three more times before mobilising to France on 22nd July 1915. The Battalion's start was not without incident. Quarter Master Sergeant A. Batkin was found dead in his billet at Quelmes on 25th July and then in August 1914, whilst undergoing instruction in trench warfare, four Riflemen were accidentally wounded and one officer killed. The first trench duty undertaken by the Battalion was in positions near to the village of Lamentie where they relieved 3rd Ghurkhas on 27th August 1915. They themselves were relieved on 2nd September and in that time, they had been targeted by sharpshooters, three men were killed and seven wounded but they had accounted for five enemy snipers.

On December 1st 1915, the Battalion relieved the front line trenches near to Fleurbaix and in this three day period the enemy were very quiet and only one man was wounded. On the 4th December 1915 Sydney was accidentally killed whilst on duty in this trench system, no record exists as to how he met his end but he was buried in Grave K23 of Y Farm Military Cemetery Bois-Grenier France. He left £5.9s.8d. supplemented by a War Gratuity of £5 to his mother, Susan, he was awarded the 1915-15 Star, Victory and British War Medals.

Chapter 28

Samuel Welbourne

All the stories involving loss of life from war are tragic and each of us beholds some we find sadder than others. Samuel Welbourne's story, for me, is one of those.

Samuel was born in Tamworth in 1889, to Joseph and Charlotte Welbourne of 1, Wheeleys Yard, Court No. 3, 87, Lichfield Street, Tamworth. Joseph worked as a Stoker at a local paper-mill and Charlotte looked after the family. Samuel was their sixth child and three years later another son was born. Between this birth and 1901, Joseph died forcing Charlotte to seek employment as a Paper Sorter at the mill. Samuel at 12, was working as a bricklayer's labourer. Samuel's mum, Charlotte, then passed away and he was adopted by Samuel and Phoebe Marklew of Birchmoor, Tamworth. Samuel Marklew was a miner by profession and Samuel Welbourne obtained employment at Pooley Hall Colliery as a Filler. The Marklews had five children of their own and the eldest son also worked as a Miner Filler.

On 3rd September 1914, Samuel attended Lichfield recruitment offices and enlisted in the army. He was posted to the Kings Liverpool Regiment as Private 18210 and completed his basic training with 4th (extra reserve) Battalion. This extra reserve Battalion was additional to the 3rd (reserve) Battalion which remained in the UK throughout the war. Both served as training units to cope with the overwhelming influx of volunteers answering the call to arms at the start of the war, but the 4th Battalion then mobilised to France in March 1915. By this time, Samuel had completed his training and been posted to 12th Battalion. Whilst at the Regiment's Seaforth camp, Samuel was given a pass to leave camp which expired at 12 midnight on 9th November 1914, he overstayed this deadline and did not return until 1st December 1914; for which offence he was fined four days' pay. This appears to be a more serious offence than the punishment awarded but he was clearly a good soldier and was promoted to Lance Corporal on 15th February 1915.

In July 1915, the Battalion were based in a camp on Salisbury Plain, Wiltshire, when the order to mobilise to the Western Front was received. On 24thJuly, at midnight, following a day's delay due to bad weather, by train, march and ship, the Battalion arrived in Boulogne and marched to a nearby camp. Following the usual training and instruction in trench warfare, the Battalion took its place in the front line in early August 1915, near to Armentières. They were soon introduced to enemy artillery and their first casualties.

Samuel spent the following months in the routine of trench relief, days at the rear followed by periods in the front line and support. On 5th May 1916, for an unexplained reason, Samuel was returned to the rank of Private at his own request. To ensure that this event was not seen in the future as detrimental to his reputation as a soldier, the Commanding Officer signed a declaration that this action had been taken at Samuel's own request and not to evade any consequences of a Court Martial as per Kings Regulations, paragraph 301.

On 20th August 1916, the Battalion entrained to the Somme area and camped at Happy Valley and, on 22nd August, they relieved 1st Battalion Royal Fusiliers in Bernafay Wood. For three days, they endured heavy shelling and suffered casualties.

On 23rd, nine men were killed and 12 wounded; the next day, 24th August 1916, the casualty count was two killed and 19 wounded of which Samuel was one. He received a shrapnel wound to his hand and was evacuated to 20 Casualty Clearing Station for treatment, the wound proved to be what was described as, 'a Blighty one' meaning that he was returned to England for hospital treatment there. On 28th August 1916, Samuel arrived back in England from France and was transported to hospital in Huddersfield.

For administrative purposes, Samuel was transferred to 3rd (Reserve) Battalion, treated at the hospital and when discharged sent to Prees Camp near to Whitchurch in Shropshire. Prees Camp had been opened in 1914 and expanded to accommodate 25,000 men, electricity was installed in the camp before the town of Whitchurch! Whilst here Samuel again had a brush with military discipline when he again failed to return to camp on time, this time he was absent from 2 p.m. 11thto 2 p.m. 14th December 1916 and on this occasion, he was dealt with far more severely by being fined 21 days' pay and was confined to barracks for 14 days.

On 5th January 1917, Samuel was transferred to 19th Battalion and returned to France arriving there on 12th January and attended a course at the Divisional School at 24th Infantry Base Depot (IBD). The 19th Battalion were in camp at Halloy, Nord-Pas-de-Calais, and engaged in training new attack techniques, use of rifle grenades, Lewis gun and target practise on the ranges. They were also regularly engaged in providing working parties for various projects.

At the beginning of February 1917, the Battalion moved to billets in the village of Agny, three miles south-west of Arras and returned to rotation duty in the trenches there. The enemy had been very quiet and the main activity was their effective use of the Minenwerfer or Trench Mortar. These were an extremely effective short-range weapon, which were used for destroying bunkers and dugouts. On 22nd February 1917, A Company HQ was subject of a direct hit, blown in and a Captain killed and Lieutenant wounded. The usual response to these attacks was by the artillery who relied on spotters to pinpoint exactly where the mortar was situated to destroy it and its crew. The British mortar crews were not always the most popular of men as they tended to draw the attention of the enemy artillery, but they were mobile units and moved location, which was not always helpful for the men situated at the vacated locations. At the end of February, the Battalion split in two; one half forming working parties and the other attending the Divisional school where they practised attack techniques, musketry and fighting with the bayonet. The evenings were spent receiving lectures, all in preparation for a planned attack. Midway through March 1917, the Battalion regrouped and went back into the line.

The attack techniques being practised were in preparation for the Second Battle of Arras which commenced on 9th April 1917, and involved 23 divisions, 14 of which lined up on the first day. The attack was preceded by an artillery bombardment using 2,689,000 shells, 1,000,000 more than used in the Somme Offensive. A creeping barrage accompanied the infantry attack, whereby artillery shells were fired to a point 100 yards in front of the advancing infantry allowing them to get very close to the enemy positions while they had their heads down. This tactic had been used before but on this occasion the practice had involved a greater emphasis on synchronicity between the component parts. The new tactics also included a new standardised attack method to be employed by the BEF and involved the combined use of riflemen, bombers, snipers and Lewis gun crews to assault individual targets and proved to be highly successful on the first day of the attack with the high ground of Vimy Ridge being captured before a stalemate situation developed. At 2 p.m. on that first day, the 19th Battalion went into action.

The 19th Battalion KLR, like all the units involved in this battle, had clearly defined objectives; the German front, second and third lines, the village of Heninel and the high ground beyond the village. The Battalion advanced on a two Company front, B and C Company lead with A and D Companies in support, with a strict schedule to adhere to. By 3 p.m. Heninel was taken and the Companies were advancing on the German front line known as the Hindenburg Line. The men came under heavy machinegun fire and an artillery barrage, most the casualties being taken were from the machineguns. By 6 p.m., these numbers had reached one officer and 50 men. At 5 p.m., the Companies had dug in due to the intensity of the fire and were within 100 yards of the German line. Initially the defensive positions created were making use of shell holes but during the evening a trench was dug connecting with the Battalions on their flanks. At midnight orders were received to withdraw to allow the artillery to bombard the German wire, giving access for a further attack. The day's casualty list was; six officers and 217 other ranks killed or wounded, of which Samuel was one of the latter. He was hit by machinegun bullets in the left arm and legs and evacuated to 20 Casualty Clearing Station and from there to 1st Canadian General Hospital at Etaples where he died from his wounds on 14th April 1917.

Samuel was buried in Etaples Military Cemetery and the business of informing relatives was undertaken, but with a complex antecedent many of his siblings were not traced for some time. Samuel left a will which left each sibling named a proportion of his estate which amounted to, £9.13s.8d supplemented by a War Gratuity of £12. Eventually his possessions and medals were forwarded to his brother, Joseph Welbourne, the medals awarded were 1914-15 Star, Victory and British War Medals.

Chapter 29

William Henry West

The West Family resided at Bridge Street, Polesworth, not far from the Pooley Hall Colliery. John Henry West was a Polesworth born man and was employed as a Hewer in the mine. His wife, Catherine, was also a local, having been born in nearby Atherstone. By 1901, Catherine had given birth to six children of which William was the fifth. He was born on 15th May 1897 and Christened at Polesworth Church on 26th September that same year. Ten years later John West, now a Widower, was still a Miner and living at the same address with his nine surviving children; the youngest child was two years old. Catherine, who had by now given birth to ten children, had died at a date following this birth. William, aged 13, had left school and was employed as a Coal Mine Labourer on the bank, his two elder brothers were also employed as Miners.

On 21st August 1914, William attested to join the army at Atherstone and was posted to the South Staffordshire Regiment,

7th Battalion, as Private 10910. His medical report states that he was a fresh-faced man. 5' 6⅜" tall, weighing 117½ lbs, with blue/grey eyes and brown hair. The 7th Battalion was formed at Lichfield in 1914 and initially that is where William commenced his basic training. The first move was to Grantham and then, in April 1915, to Frensham. William completed basic training and volunteered for the newly formed Army Cyclist Corps. On 1st March 1915, he was transferred to that Corps and his army number changed to 4916. On 7th May 1915, William attended a course of instruction in artificer ordinance, passed and was awarded a certificate. This would appear to be an introductory phase to the issue of dealing with ordinance and probably involved safe handling and storage.

The army cyclists at this stage of the war were a Divisional resource and both William's cyclist unit and 7th Battalion South Staffordshire Regiment, were part of 11th (Northern) Division. Early in July 1915, 7th Battalion embarked for Gallipoli from Liverpool, whilst on 1st July 1915, William boarded the HT (Hired Transport) Ascaria at Devonport also bound for the same destination. On 19th August 1915, William was assigned to the 11th Signal Company as an Orderly for ten days, but after two days back with his unit he was returned to the same Signal Company until 28th September when he again re-joined his unit. On 15th October 1915 William was promoted to Lance Corporal.

In December 1915, both 7th South Staffs and William as part of 11th Division, were evacuated from Gallipoli to Egypt. In June 1916, William embarked at Alexandria on the HT Oriana bound for France to join the B.E.F. there, his old Battalion, 7th South Staffs, followed the next month, July.

On 19th January 1917, the 11th, 19th and 62nd Divisional Cyclists were formed as a single unit, now known as 18th Corps Cyclist Battalion based at Pas-de-Calais and a War Diary commenced.

The men were divided into three Companies. A Company, which William was assigned to, comprised six officers and 134 other ranks; B Company, four officers and 94 other ranks and C Company, nine officers and 193 other ranks. Command was assumed by Captain W.B. Litherland with 2nd Lieutenant R. Sidney employed as Adjutant. The rest of the month was spent supplying working parties to the Royal Engineers, improving billets, training and inspections. Towards the end of February, William was granted leave and returned to the England to be reunited with his family for a few weeks, this was the first time he had seen them since embarking for foreign shores in December 1915.

On his return the Company was a little more organised, billets had been erected and duties expanded, in addition to the working parties, the cyclists were now also employed on traffic control and orderly duties. Regular physical training sessions were held for those not assigned to specific duties to maintain and improve personal fitness. In July 1917, William was granted class one proficiency pay. Training schedules were set on a regular basis and included in the programme were; physical training, parades with the cycles to practise mounting, dismounting and ride discipline, close order drill, musketry including training to judge distance, bayonet fighting, giving orders on the move and controlling cycle columns.

During September 1917, the cyclists were engaged in 'Chinese Attacks', this involved the making of soldier silhouettes, both standing and kneeling, and then used in the field to deceive the enemy as to where an attack was to be launched. The men crawled to positions in shell craters and raised the figures for a few seconds at a time to draw enemy fire, the third time this was done, on 26th September, 280 figures were used successfully drawing fire from artillery and machine guns. This duty was not without danger, during the attack on 26th, one officer, five other ranks and a RAMC stretcher bearer were wounded and one other rank was killed.

On 24th March 1918, William left his unit for leave in England to spend some time with his family back in Tamworthand did not return until 5th April. Shortly after his return to duty, on 20th April 1918, William was promoted Corporal.

With the increasing use of aeroplanes, by both sides as the war progressed, there became a greater need for ground defences, the cyclists were trained in the use of the Lewis gun for this purpose and between 25th May and 12th June 1918, William attended a Lewis Gun course to participate in this duty.

At 11 p.m. on 16th June 1918, near to Camblain-l'Abbé, William was assigned to a working party of one officer and 11 men, in a gravel quarry in front of the British line. The work was of a special nature and involved the positioning of camouflage to obscure the enemy's vision of a forthcoming gas attack. The work drew the attention of the enemy who attacked the position with trench mortars, the Lieutenant, Sergeant with two other men were wounded and one man, Private 4915 Fred Barnes was killed. William was now in charge, he decided to continue the work, the wounded being removed from the field to safety. At 2 a.m., the German mortars again pounded their positions and three more men were injured. Down to four men, William decided to abandon the work incomplete and get the wounded to safety. With the intention of recovering Fred Barnes's body, William and three of the remaining men left cover to retrieve him, they had almost achieved their objective when another mortar shell hit their position and William was killed instantly. The remainder of the working party retired to safety with the wounded and both dead men. William and Fred had joined the 18th Cyclist unit together as their numbers were consecutive and no doubt good friends, both men were later buried side by side in Maroc British Cemetery, Grenay (Graves 111. A 3 and 4).

William left £7.8s.2d. supplemented by a War Gratuity of £19 to his father, John, who was also sent his possessions, a wallet, watch, cigarette case, key, some photos and a lanyard. William was awarded the 1914-15 Star, Victory and British War Medals.

Chapter 30

Clive Williams

Clive was born in Langley, Oldbury, on 18th May 1894, the third child of Levi and Amplias Williams. In 1901, the family were living at Myrtle Cottage, Waterfall Lane, Rowley Regis. Levi was a builder, Carpenter and contractor and ran his own business employing several people. Clive's elder sister, Henrietta aged 18, was employed as a 'Board School Teacher', which would indicate that the family were reasonably well off to be able to afford an education for their daughter. In 1911, Henrietta was still single, employed as an elementary school Teacher and living with her mother and Clive at 4, Watling Street, Wilnecote, Tamworth. Levi Williams had passed away and presumably, Clive's education had been curtailed as a result. He was working as a Labourer at Kingsbury Colliery but at some stage between 1911 and 1916, Clive changed employers and worked as a Labourer at the Pooley Hall Colliery, in Polesworth.

In 1917, probably towards the end of the year, Clive enlisted in the British Army at Tamworth and was inducted into the Royal Warwickshire Regiment as Private 57334; aged 21, he was almost certainly a conscript. The only surviving records show that he served with the 1/8thBattalion but the Regiment had two reserve Battalions, the 3rd and 4th which in 1917, were based on the Isle of Wight and where all new recruits to the Regiment were initially sent for basic training.

The 1/8th Battalion Royal Warwickshire Regiment was formed in Aston Cross, Birmingham, in August 1914 in response to the incredible response to the call to arms following the outbreak of World War I. The Battalion was sent to France on 21st March 1915 and landed at Le Havre the following day. In May 1915, the Battalion was assigned to 143rd Brigade, 48th (South Midland) Division, which moved to Italy in November 1917 and then returned to France on 11th September 1918 as part of 75th Brigade, 25th Division.

Prior to World War I, Italy was a member of the Triple Alliance with Austria-Hungary and Germany, but did not declare war with its allies in 1914 claiming that the war was a defensive issue and there was no need for Italy to be involved. From the start of the war and early 1915, Italy was courted by the diplomats of the Entente Cordiale (Allies) and in May 1915 signed The Treaty of London. On 23rd May 1915, Italy declared war on neighbouring Austria-Hungary. The war between the two countries was fought along the borders; for the most part, in the mountains of the Alps. Some of the front extended down onto the plains north of Venice, which were mosquito infested swamps. In 1917, British forces were removed from the fighting of the Third Battle of Ypres and transported down through France into Italy to support the Italian Army. Leaving the rain, mud, flooded trenches and slaughter of this part of Flanders to travel south for days by train, the weather gradually getting warmer and drier must have been a huge relief for Clive and his travel companions, not to mention the excitement of seeing foreign and strange lands.

The 1/8th Battalion's War Diary for September 1918 shows that they were holding the line at a place described as Plateau; this was no doubt a name for a location in the Alpine Mountains. Here the trench warfare which had developed was not an ordered and planned system, the positions were hewn out of solid rock and every available rock fault or fissure had been used to blast a trench system to protect the soldiers holding the line there. Caves were used or created using explosives as there were no dugouts as created on the Western front. The usual artillery exchanges between the opposing forces created a further danger. As well as the usual metal shrapnel created by an exploding shell, the limestone tended to add to the injuries caused with flying shards of rock of varying sizes.

The Treaty of Brest-Litovsk, signed on 3rd March 1918 between the new Soviet Government of Russia and the Central Powers, had ended Russia's involvement in World War I and thereby released 50 German divisions which could be redeployed to the Western Front. The German Spring Offensive of 1918, known as the Ludendorff Offensive, had driven the Western Front further back than any other advances initiated by either side since 1914. The intention was to break the stalemate on this front and deliver a killer blow before the might of the Forces of the USA could be deployed to great effect. The Offensive failed and in response the Allied forces had mounted a counter offensive with the intention of destroying the German armies on the Western Front. It was decided to reinforce British Divisions by removing forces from the Italian Front and on 13thSeptember 1918, incidentally a Friday, orders were received by 1/8th Battalion HQ to entrain for return to France. The Battalion had moved to a town called Centrale on route to take over positions on the plains, so new orders to return to France may have been a mixed bag to the men who had experienced the awful conditions prevailing in the trenches at that time of year, but the Plains held their own hazards in the swamps, with mosquito bites causing Malaria.

Two trains took Clive and his companions via the Riviera Route to France and was completed on 19th September 1918. When they arrived at St Riquer, they detrained and marched to Yvrencheux near Abbeville Northern France. The Battalion trained for a few days with attention being paid to the Lewis

Gun and they were inspected by their Brigadier on 26th September 1918. A further train journey took them to where they were to go into the line around Albert and then days of marching brought them to the front line at Lormisett, arriving on 5th October 1918. The Battalion was split, two Companies to support the Sherwood Foresters in their attack on a German strong Point at Guisancourt Farm, and two Companies to support the Yorkshire Regiment at Belle Ville Farm. The diary describes the advance of the Companies to their respective positions as superb under heavy machine gun and artillery fire but does not state whether there were any casualties as a result.

By 7th October both halves of the Battalion had assembled at Lormisett and returned to the control of the Battalion Commander, Lieutenant Colonel Whitehouse. From here the Battalion went into action at Sonia Farm where it held the line between the 30th American Division and the 7th Brigade. A series of engagements of varying sizes then occurred over the next few weeks and are best summarised from the diary:

9th October 1918, zero hour 5.20 a.m. the objective beyond Maretz taken by 6.30 a.m.

10th October 1918, zero hour 5.30 a.m. Battalion advanced and engaged in heavy fighting on the outskirts of Le Cateau but due to the Americans being held up further advance was not possible. Positions taken consolidated and held.

11th October relieved from front line, casualties during this period; 1 officer and 24 Other Ranks killed, 5 officers and 163 Other Ranks wounded.

18th October 1918, returned to the front line at Honnechy and in support by Company as needed to the Worcester and Gloster (Gloucester) Regiments.

19ᵗʰ October 1918, as 18ᵗʰ.

20ᵗʰ October 1918, as 18ᵗʰ at 8.30 p.m. relieved from the front line. During this period 3 Other Ranks killed, 27 Other Ranks wounded.

23ʳᵈ October, engaged in action at Pommereuil as support to the 9ᵗʰ Devon Regiment. The attack commenced at 1.20 a.m. in heavy fog and front line units became mixed up and missed machine gun nests which then became very effective against the support Battalion. This situation was resolved by an experienced officer of the 1/8ᵗʰ Battalion (Captain Mortimore M.C.) and all objectives were eventually achieved.

24ᵗʰ October 1918, attack continued as per day before and at 10.53 a.m. they held their positions until units of the 7ᵗʰ Brigade has passed through and relieved them, they then retired to billets at Pommereuil. Casualties during this period; 13 Other Ranks killed, 5 Other Ranks missing, 3 officers and 40 Other Ranks wounded.

During the next few days the Battalion continued training and a draft of 143 Other Ranks was absorbed. On 30ᵗʰ October, the Companies trained but also had opportunity for a bath. On 31ˢᵗ October 1918, the Battalion relieved the 11ᵗʰ Sherwood Foresters in the front line at Le Faux. Between 1ˢᵗ and 7ᵗʰ November 1918, the Battalion was engaged in attacking the German positions to their front. They experienced heavy opposition and during this period the casualties were; one officer and 27 other ranks killed and two officers and 106 other ranks wounded. On 8ᵗʰ November 1918, the Battalion marched out to billets at Preux-au-Bois, their war was over as they trained and cleaned in preparation for a return to the front but on 11ᵗʰ November 1918 the Armistice came into force and at 11 a.m. the guns fell silent. The diary for that day just says; *'Training'*!

On 20th November 1918 Clive Williams succumbed to his wounds and passed away in No.12 General Hospital in Rouen France. Due to the loss of his personal file we do not know when he received his wounds and what they were, but we do know that he was one of the casualties as mentioned in the actions above and due to the distance from Rouen to the front line his wounds were likely to have been incurred on 10th or 11thOctober, when 163 men were wounded.

Clive's death was reported in the Tamworth Herald, the newspaper local to where he worked and his family lived, it simply stated;

57334 Pte.Clive Williams 1/8 Royal Warwicks, aged 25 (of Wilnecote), died of wounds received in action on November 20, 1918 at No. 12 General Hospital, Rouen.

Clive left £9.8s.0d. to his mother, Amplias, which was supplemented by a War Gratuity of £5 (Indicating a late 1917 joining date). The authorisation for settlement of this account was not made until 18th March 1919. He was awarded the British War and Victory Medals for his ultimate sacrifice and he was laid to rest in St Sever Cemetery Extension, Rouen.

Chapter 31

Brothers Samuel and Percy Willis

Many in Britain experienced the loss of multiple family members, but the loss to the family of the Willis brothers, was exceptionally severe as the dates of death were so close as to deny the family any recovery period between the two losses.

Samuel was the elder of the two boys, born at 23, Bridge Street, Polesworth, in 1892, three years before Percy, who was born on 24 Nov 1895, at the same address. Their father was Thomas Henry Willis, a coal miner employed as a Hewer, and Elizabeth Willis, a local girl from Wilnecote, Tamworth. In total, Elizabeth bore14 children of which, by 1911, 11 had survived. It would appear that all the boys in the family followed their father into the coal mining industry and left school at the earliest opportunity at the age of 12 in order to do so. In 1911, Samuel was employed as a Coal Miner Day Man (underground) and Percy, at the age of 15, was employed as a Coal Miner on a haulage train (underground).

Neither men's military files have survived, but piecing the available information together we can say that at the outbreak of war Samuel was aged 22 and Percy aged 20. Samuel's eligibility for medals occurred when he landed in France on 24th August 1915, and Percy's date is unknown but after 1st January 1916. Both men's records show they were, at one time or another, posted to two different Battalions of the same regiment and none of the dates actually coincide with the mobilisation of the Battalions they were serving with when they died. This may be because the dates available are wrong or they travelled independently of their respective units and arrived as additional personnel.

Samuel Willis, Private 15850, served with both 9th and 1/6th Battalions South Staffordshire Regiment. He entered France on 24th August 1915 and was killed in action on 16th May 1918, fighting with the 1/6th. At the beginning of May 1918, the 1/6th Battalion was rotating in the front line trenches with 1/5th Battalion South Staffordshire regiment in the vicinity of Essars near to Bethune. They had been on the receiving end of a heavy gas shell bombardment for the first two days of the month until they were relieved and moved into reserve at Vaudricourt Wood. Here they rested in tented accommodation and bathed. Between 6th and 10th May 1918, the 1/6th again spent time in the front line but on this occasion it was quiet, an expected attack by the enemy did not materialise. Following two days in reserve the 1/6th again went into the front line until relieved on 14th May when they went to rest billets at Verquin. This was seemingly a safe location to rest, clean and recover strength and nerve. At 2.30 a.m. on 16th May 1918, the German artillery shelled the camp achieving direct hits on the billets occupied by B and D Companies, five men were killed and 21 wounded. Unfortunately Samuel was one of those killed; he may well have been asleep and never knew what hit him. The wounded were evacuated to medical facilities and the survivors of these two companies went into the tented accommodation of Vaudricourt Wood.

Samuel was buried in grave 1.C.18 at Houchin British Cemetery. He left £12.8s.2d, supplemented by a War Gratuity of £16.10s.0d to his father, Thomas and he was subsequently awarded the 1915-15 Star, British War and Victory Medals.

Samuel's family were notified and his death reported in the Tamworth Herald on 15th June 1918.

Percy Willis served with both 14th and 2/7th Battalions, Royal Warwickshire Regiment, entered France after 1st January 1916 and was killed in action on 24th October 1918, only six months after his brother Samuel, whilst serving with the 2/7th. During October 1918, Percy's Battalion were in billets to the South of Cambrai. The 1918 Battle of Cambrai was successfully over but fighting was still ongoing in this area and Percy was in the thick of it. Whilst in these billets the Battalion was undergoing training specifically designed for the forthcoming attack on the German line planned for 24th October 1918. On 23rd October, the Battalion marched to their first designated assembly point, a wood near to Montrecourt, where they rested until 9.45 p.m., they then moved across country to their start position arriving at 3.15 a.m. At 4 a.m. the advance to the village of Sommaing started, the Battalion's dispositions being, X and Z company leading, with Percy's Y Company in immediate support and W Company in reserve. An artillery barrage commenced and when the Companies attacked, they were met with heavy machinegun fire and by 10 a.m. Y Company had moved forward in support of X Company but both were pinned down by the German guns. The Battalion fought in these positions until 4.45p.m., 24th October 1918 and they were then relieved when the 2/8th Worcester Regiment passed through their lines to press the attack afresh. The Battalion moved to Brigade support and the head count on 25th October was; 22 officers and 503 other ranks; the casualties occurring on 24th October were, four officers killed and one officer wounded by gas. Other rank casualties are merely listed as 198, which included Percy who was killed. The successes on the day were; 150 prisoners, one 77mm field gun, nine machineguns and one anti-tank gun captured. The Battalion stayed in a support role until the end of May when their head count was recorded as; 20 officers and

436 other ranks, the casualties had continued even out of the front line!

Percy's body was subsequently recovered, identified and buried in grave B. 14 of Canonne Farm British Military Cemetery near to the village of Sommaing. His family again suffered the anguish of a missing report and then a further death message with insufficient time to grieve for their other son, Samuel. Percy left £7.6s.2d supplemented by a War Gratuity of £5 (Indicating service of approximately one year), also to his father Thomas, and he was awarded the British War and Victory Medals.

Chapter 32

Conclusion

With the mobilisation of American troops to the Western Front in 1917, the failure of the German Spring Offensive of 1918 and the pressure applied by the allies in the ensuing counter offensive, the German high command decided the War could not be won and made overtures to end the fighting. A ceasefire was agreed to commence from 11 a.m. 11th November 1918, but the carnage continued during the countdown to the appointed time. Men of all sides continued to be killed or injured by all the methods devised during this terrible conflict until the very last minute.

Very few Battalion war diaries mention the ceasefire other than in a passing note and there is no mention of great celebration in the trenches. To the men at the front it was just a ceasefire and not the end of the war. When the guns went silent many men were assigned to fatigues to start repairing roads and the damage of war. Cities, towns and villages throughout Belgium and eastern France were destroyed and would take many years to restore them to their former glory and some were never rebuilt. The countryside had been transformed from beautiful rolling fields and woodland into a maze of trenches, bunkers and strongpoints. The war underground had created a labyrinth of tunnels, galleries and bunkers, which were sealed and forgotten, but every now and again we are reminded of their existence when a hole appears, usually when a tractor's weight is over a weak point. Those same tractors unearth tons of ordnance every year, of all types; shrapnel, high explosive and gas. The farmers carry these dangerous items to the roadside where they are collected and disposed of by experts. The detritus of war is still endangering innocent people even after 100 years and that is largely due to the high volume of artillery shells which had failed to explode. Underground galleries charged with high explosive were often abandoned and sealed; the explosive does deteriorate over time, but is safer left in situ rather than risk moving it to a suitable disposal place.

On 11th November 1918 the guns went silent, but this did not in itself end the war. In the City of Versailles, negotiations commenced between the protagonists, which ultimately resulted in the treaty of Versailles being agreed and signed on 28th June 1919 (exactly 5 years from the assassination of Archduke Franz Ferdinand) and this is the actual end date of World War 1. This treaty punished the Germans punitively as her colonies in Africa were confiscated and the country was subjected to huge financial reparations to pay for the damage caused in France and Belgium.

The Royal households of Europe fell, except for Britain's. In 1917 King George V, in response to anti-German feeling, changed the name of his royal house from Saxe-Coburg and Gotha to Windsor. He had also spent a lot of time supporting and visiting troops both at home and the front. Queen Mary had been very active with initiatives to support nursing and the troops including the Christmas tin in 1914. Needless to say the propaganda machine had been active creating postcards and other pictorial media to ensure a positive image of the Royal work. 100 years later the House of Windsor is still a much loved institution with many Royal heirs in the line of succession. Kaiser Wilhelm entered self imposed exile the day before the armistice and never returned to Germany and

Russia's Tsar Nicholas had been murdered along with his whole family following the 1917 Russian Revolution.

The war ending in this manner for many Germans was a matter of national disgrace, particularly for one lowly Austrian Corporal named Adolf Hitler, who had received the news whilst recovering from the effects of gas in a military hospital. His bitterness and hatred became a driving force and he determined to do anything to right what he saw as Germany being 'stabbed in the back' by politicians at home and international Jewry. The ensuing world recession of the late 20's and 30's was particularly bad for Germany, which was struggling to repay the reparations imposed on them and suffering out of control inflation. Those lucky to have employment were carrying their wages home in wheelbarrows and a loaf of bread cost millions of 'marks. People's savings and the wealth of the middle classes were made worthless, creating a general feeling of malcontent and a breeding ground for extreme political support. A struggle for power existed between the far left and right with the centre parties fighting to create a balance and democracy. By various means including violence, perpetuation of the myths created by Hitler's personal hatreds and undermining the democratic process from within, the Nazi Party gained power and created a dictatorship under Hitler, the path for global conflict was set and inevitable.

World War 2, as far as it affected Europe, concluded with a signed unconditional surrender on 8th May 1945 and many believe that this was finally the conclusion of World War 1.

About the Author

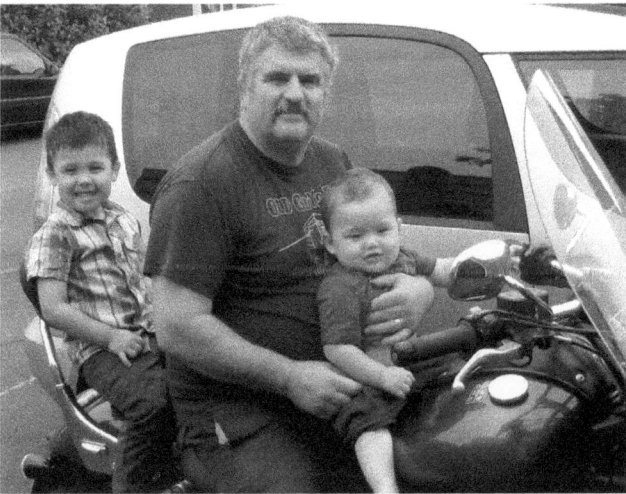

Mick is a retired British police officer having served in both Birmingham City and West Midlands forces. He served in both uniform, CID and other specialist units gaining experience and expertise in major investigation. In retirement he has combined two lifelong passions, motorcycling and history, resulting in research trips throughout Western Europe and books about the two World Wars.

A member and supporter of the Royal British Legion royalties from this book will donated to that worthy cause.

Lightning Source UK Ltd.
Milton Keynes UK
UKHW010609280120
357692UK00001B/77

9 781786 232069